TECONOMICS OF OF VERBALISM OF VERBALISM

Bahman Fakhraie, Ph.D.

TECONOMICS OF VERBALISM

By

Dr. Bahman Fakhraie

September 3, 2012

Front and back cover, FERDAT
FERDAT Publishing, Ogden, UT, USA
Published in Untied States of America
Library of Congress 1827588
United States Dollar 89.99
Bar Code Price Tag 58999

$89.99
ISBN 978-0-9852958-4-4
58999>
780985 295844

ABSTRACT

In this study, the syllabication advances the syllogism of supply and demand causations of technological injection and shifts of exponential increase in words usage in United States of America for 1900 to 2015. This is researched under Teconmics of Verbalism.

The Teconmics of Verbalism synthesizes that the trifurcated forces of governances, finance, and economic markets and their global technological interdependencies have exerted inordinate forces to shape societal constructs, in modern times. It is very important to garnish this study and research at this holistic unorthodox economic level. Because the elemental resources employment and utilization aspects introduced in this study are widely applied, and they have obtained global prominence and importance. They are different from the bloviated-exaggerated verbigeration that inundates and under serves humanity in different formats. The income elasticity and mathematical studies of elemental aspect of Gross Domestic Product, or an estimation of nominal and real summation of economic activities, in GDP growth, and money velocities are applied, in order to elevate comprehensions of vital fields of modern new field of teconometric studies. These are part of Dr. Bahman Fakhraie's research, which have been initiated since middle of 1970s. They have been presented in different presentations, and book publications.

Therefore, the value theory of economic variables and conditions, which influence the aggregated data in fiscal economics, can become comprehensible to the practitioners in all three fields. It is important to realize scientific bases beyond verbigeration that will serve to construct our future systems on firmer foundations, stronger than words of conflicts, with structures, organizational coordination, planning, and leaderships to accomplish the constructional sustainable relations, which will engender sustainable economic progress.

The millennial economic events evolved during thirty years of wealth concentration strategies, misrepresented as wealth-building-alternative roads to prosperity. There have been under cuttings and negative currents, instead of combined efforts to push ahead in unison globally, or regionally. These were presented as inclusive of all Americans, with positive externalities to push or adopt austerity as part of a constructive futuristic package of technological injections in order to maintain an inclusive economic growth path. Therefore, why not do the right things initially?

CONTENTS

LIST OF FIGURES

Figures Pages

DEDICATION

To Kay Davis, Lara Fatemeh, Anayat Wayne.

To those at work, (sometime in hazardous duties)

for peace, health, and prosperity of humanity,

moreover, to those in education globally.

CHAPTER 1

TECONOMICS OF VERBALISM

This is a teconomic analysis of words usage and media technologies from 1900 to 2015. In this study the expansion of verbiages in technology are explained in terms of teconomic analysis.[1] It will be noted in details associated with growth and development of technologies related to media growth in word usage, as well as, the exponential expansion in usage of words.

However, it is quite different, when these became a political radical rights' exclusionary agenda, mixed with overt racial overtones, anti-women politics, anti-minority agenda, a southern strategy push against all immigrants, (hoping they will force them illegally and unconscionably to self deport), and a vehicle of war profiteering for foreign intrigues and opportunists' wish lists. Then, the higher income tax revenues to get on the corrective economic counter-cyclical path were undermined, by the main beneficiaries of the same plans. Even small percentages or honest adjustments were postponed. Worst, the wrong ideas took the rungs out of the economic growth and development ladder for the middle class workers, for new graduates already overburdened by usurious and commercialized student loans schemes, for the chronically poor, under-employed, and unemployed. Then, they turned the policies beneficial externalities focus upwards for three decades of wealth concentrations. They wanted to fee and tax the middle class, cut the education of their children, cut their social security (and SSI), and raise their benefit collection ages, and cut the middle class Medicare to their retiring parents, while they are cutting their jobs. All the while, they were howling class warfare. They are astonished about the political pushback and democratic backlash, and voters' revolt. This is still marginally at their expense, not punitively, and unfairly, yet. Nevertheless, they are not finished. They are mistakenly reloading. Unhappily, the consequences will become larger unattended, because the concentration of wealth rather than wealth-jobs creation will revisit them, too. These policies have had real financial victims and real consequences, and their victims will victimize them back, if they bother to skim history of modern democracies. Do the right thing initially, and take the dynamic corrective steps incrementally, they prove to be the economically prudent choices.

INTRODUCTION

Some definition of terms and principles used in this study are presented here to assist. The synthesis of trifurcated forces of governances, finance, and economic markets and their global technological interdependencies have exerted inordinate forces in modern times, globally. It is very important to garnish this study and research equal to their global prominence and importance. Therefore, the value theory of economic variables and conditions, which influence the aggregated data in fiscal economics, can become comprehensible to the practitioners in all three fields. It is important to realize scientific bases beyond verbigeration that will serve to construct our future systems on firmer foundations stronger than words of conflicts, with structures, organizational coordination and planning, and leadership to accomplish the constructional sustainable relations.

The Political Teconomic terms are explained in more detailed in that book.[2] Stable systems are looking at economic conditions, which allow shorter-term political changes to occur for more political and economic functionalities in response to, periodic transformations, and cyclical requirements. Optimal conditions are defined as arithmetic sets of equilibriums and political stable game settlements, and Nash equilibriums, which hold stable for a period. Optimality is also a pre-requisite for Sustainability. Sustainability is defined as functionality of two, three, or more sets, economical, financial, and political equilibriums, which allow long-term adoptive and constructive changes to stabilize, without major capital destructions or bloodsheds.

The use of mathematical economics are not obvious to none economists. Nevertheless, there are some knowledge of mathematics, which is required to comprehend fully the propositional presentations, at graduate level of economics and finance. Understanding of algebraic equations, differential and integral calculus, the use of differentials and Lagrange equations, their related equities and inequalities, econometrics and statistical analysis are needed to fully utilize the presentation of preliminary books, like Teconomics, Teconometrics, and Political Teconometrics books series, and Dr. Fakhraie's dissertation discussed here leading to formal analytic studies.[3]

Therefore, the readers in this study are spared those arithmetical representations. They are not mandatory for beginners in economics, finance, and political consumers of this reads. However, they can follow the arithmetic poetry in those books series at their leisure.

TECONOMICS OF VERBALISM

The cutural technologies associated that led to book printing up to 1300 were presented.[4] The diffusion of paper was noted, from China, to Persia, to Middle East, Northern Africa, and southern and central Europe.[5] Speed of the diffusion of these related technologies were on pre-established path of information, knowledge, algebra, writing, and trade routes, which were presented by Dr. Bahman Fakhraie.[6] In this study, we see words related technologies in prints beyond books, in person and mobiles, in media and multimedia have expanded substantially.

Table 1 shows the expansion of words in different media used in trillion words estimated per years, since 1900.

Table1. Data for words in media technologies 1900-2015.

Year	Trillion words per year	Years verbiages doubled
1910	2000	-
1963	4000	53
2000	8000	37
2015	16000*	15

Calculated and graphed by Dr Fakhraie, 8-28-12
Data with (*) shows estimated value.
Mckinsey report in Economist, "Americans are exchanging ever more words"
http://www.economist.com/blogs/graphicdetail/2012/08/daily-chart-5.
Aug 22nd 2012, 14:07 by The Economist online

The exponential increase in words used in modern communicative technologies, especially as used in modern democratically oriented states, and free market oriented economies are focus of this study.[7] The aspen of words in prints, in personnel exchanges in letter, in modern television, and radio, have been augmented in intra linkages of computer communications and digital advancement.

Aside from the current political-focus in United States elections, which has garnished around an estimated one billion for each of bifurcated political side? There are multibillion dollars enterprisers in television, cable, content, digital marketing, education, and related industries forming service industries, which supply private and government jobs to growing populations.

This new data and the analysis give us an occasion to update the academic comprehensions in terms of shifts in technological advancements in supply and demand, which has allowed a democratic powerhouse around use of words in Untied States.

Figure 1 shows numbers of words used in different media estimated for each year (1910-2015).

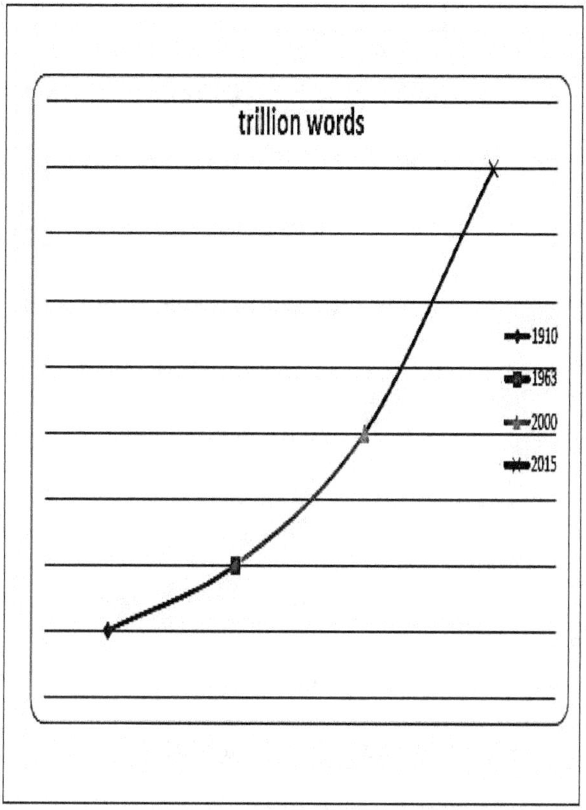

Figure 1, Trillion words and technologies of verbalism.

The 12,000 trillion-words per year of technological leaps and the means of presentation of those words are a lot. This proposes a study of technological advancements in terms of supply and demand, which make this extraordinary expansive explosion of verbiages possible.

This shows the intensity of technological injections and innovational forces at work in these expanding industries. While it if often studies as service industry, it entails innovational engineering, electronic, code writing and computer languages, and content writing far beyond its original fields of development.

Therefore, it potential for job creation and economic development and growth are also larger. The following two graphs show how much these technological advancements have become prevalent in modern society and democratic political institutions. There are legitimate complaints about campaign tactics and verbal abuse, and substantial waste of resources, skills, and financial capitals, and how and where to put 2-4 billion dollars to better use. There are in the longer run, technological progress and some employment associated with verbegtrations, and some financial infusions in small media companies in remote localities.

Figure 2 shows years it took words usage to double, and figure 3 shows the increase in demand for and supply of media technologies associated with these substantial increases in word usage over time.

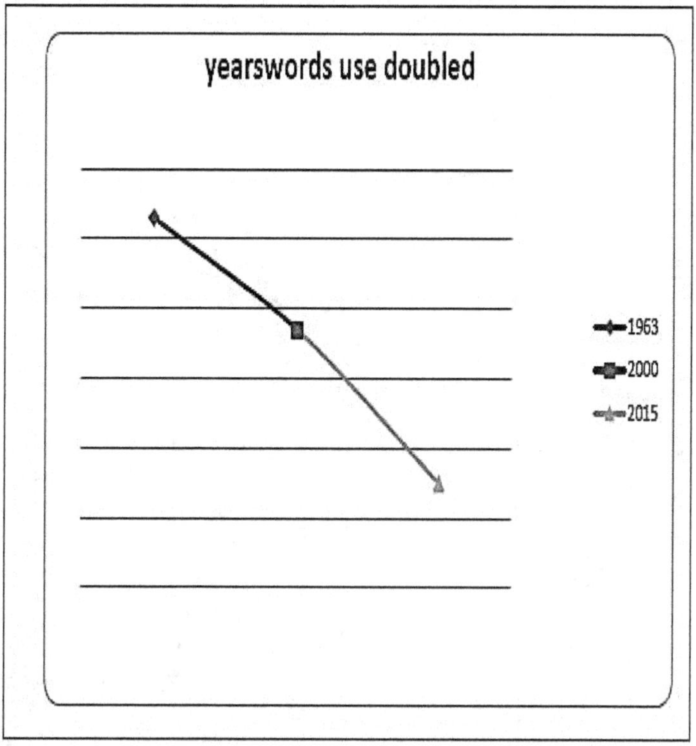

Figure 2, Number of years that words used are doubled.

D&S shifts in words use technologies

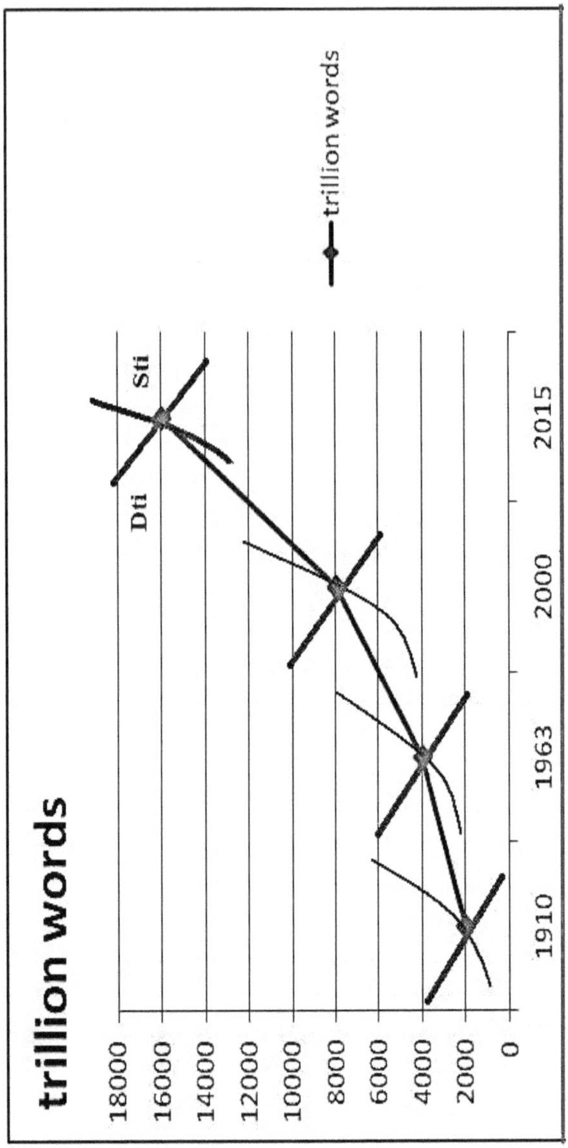

Figure 3, Technological demand and supply shifts for modern media word usage in United States 1900-2015.

TECHNOLOGCAL INJECTIONS AND JOB CREATIONS

For more detailed economic analysis of shifts in technologies (supply and demand of technologies), which relates the interconnectivities rather than the sophomoric, trite, and short-term supply-side explanations associated with these developments. Figure 4 shows the shifts in demand and supply of media-technologies associated with higher word usages. Furthermore, the political economic forces associated with such development are deterministic in the longer run developments, and are presented in Dr. Fakhraie's upcoming and new book (Political Teconomics).

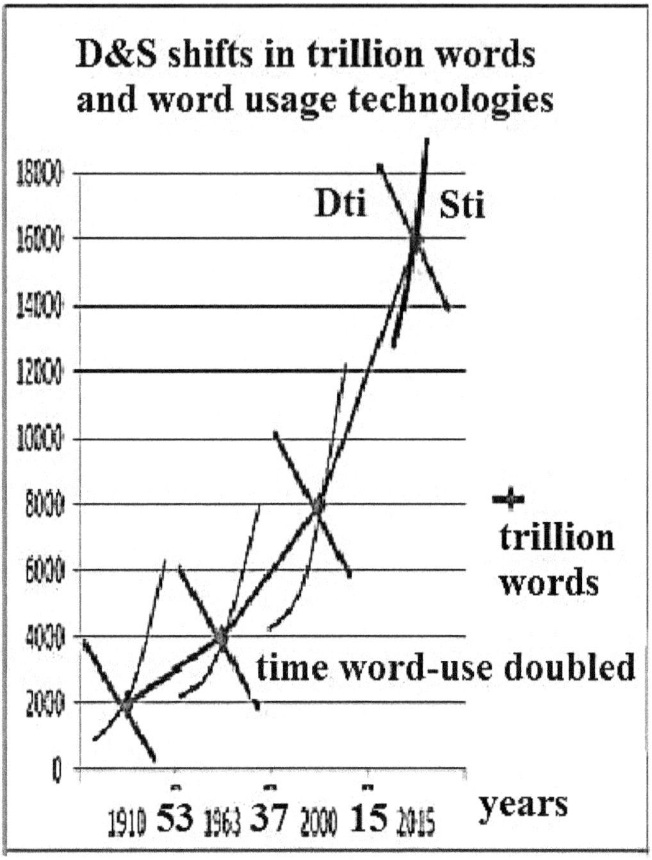

Figure 4, Technological demand and supply shifts.

For Dti to expand and induce shifts in the competitive supply side, the level of living had to have expanded accordingly.[8] However, for the second of half of the millennium the stagnant real disposable income requests alternative explanations. The important demand side issue is that the demands for words had sustained over time.

The supplied shifts are reflective of technological injection in all forms of media presentations of words. The causal result is the increase in presentational avenues for cheaper initial costs, and access fees per words. Another explanation is that post computerization. Therefore, the digital production costs per word have declined as well. The main sources of verbalism, in persons, in print-mediums, in television, radio, are the perennial technologies supplied still in full force. The expanding area of supply technologies are e-mail, internet, mobiles, the digital multimedia and social networks are gaining substantially, and pinching from the perennial mediums. They have proven to hold sway in global political liberalization anew. All intellectuals, scholars, professors, teachers, and educators, political leaders, well-read thinkers, and casual observers, are discovering its consequences moment-to-moment, alike. Humanity is best counseled to hold on to dear old humanizing principles and values, de-escalation of war mongerings, and re-employment of human skills and diplomacy. We can easily invite bigger catastrophes that we can master.

NOTES

[1] Dr. Bahman Fakhraie, *TECONOMICS, THE MICROECONOIC ANALYSIS, Scientific Synthesis of Microeconomics, mathematics and statistical, methodologies and technological parameters in production in Teconomics,* Utah Ferdat Publishing, 2012

[2] Ibid

[3] Check curriculum vita, or internet for Dr. Bahman Fakhraie's current books. Two new titles Political Teconometrics and Teconometrics will be available for publications soon.

[4] Dr. Bahman Fakhraie, *Technological Injection, Dynamic New Capital Measurements and Production theory in Economics*, Utah, Ferdat Publishing 2012 https://order.proquest.com/OA_HTML/pqdtibeCCtpItmDspRte.jsp

[5] Ibid

[6] Ibid

[7] Mckinsey, "Americans are exchanging ever more words" http://www.economist.com/blogs/graphicdetail/2012/08/daily-chart-5, Aug 22nd 2012, 14:07,The *Economist* online

[8] Dr. Bahman Fakhraie, *The Demand and Supply Side s of Technological Injections*, Utah, Ferdat Publishing 2004

CHAPTER 2

TECONOMICS OF TECHNOLOGIAL INTERDEPENDENCIES OF VERBALISM

The complexities of the trifurcated governances, finance, and economic markets and their global technological interdependencies have exerted inordinate forces in modern lives, globally.[1] It is very important to garnish studies and research equal to their global implications. There has been ritualistic rules and practices established to accommodate these interdependencies. For examples, companies do not disclose bad news, and the markets prefer negative economic projections are withheld or postponed, until after the local stock markets are closed. Therefore, equities trading start after the bad news are analyzed, and they are digested. The same difficulties with bad news will complicate campaigns in democracies.

GOVERNANCES, FINANCE, MARKETS, AND TECHNOLOGIAL INTERDEPENDENCIES OF VERBALISM

The basic laws as outputs of the sausage making machinery of the functional democracies are the byproducts of those trifurcated complexities. These practical laws allow for research and fair use act for knowledge advancement, and constitutional right for advancement of commerce and property right laws and timely adjudication of trespass, plagiarisms, theft against private property. They encourage maintenance of market-rewards (remunerations) with the original creators of contents rather than the cooperate media-manipulators.

Therefore, freedom of speech, and copyright acts are foundational injected technologies themselves. They propagate the invisible golden hidden hands to perpetuate, sometime broken dysfunctional arrangement of classic economic orthodoxy.[2] However, misapplications of statecraft verbigeration have also consequential negative externalities.

They constitute some of dangerous misapplications of technologies of verbalisms, and examples of harmful verbigeration. They are the direct correlations between accumulated concentrated power and the magnitude of inflected economy and collateral harm on resources of a society. Once again, because of steroidal technological boosters, whatever bench markers quantification are applied, they quickly and exponentially explode. Those constitute wise council and wiser correcting actions.

DANGEROUS MISSAPLICATION OF VERBALISM

One of the worst examples of modern times about dangerous misapplications of verbalism has been the expansive technology-injections of verbalism in war crafts. Their statement of causes, legality, and legitimacy are often proven dishonest and erroneous casus belli, which diminishes all democracies as governance options. Those add to the speed and potency of post war psychosis. Some Western states, unfortunately not quiet uniquely, are self-delusional about the tenants of democratic governances. Especially about war craft, they are notorious, if not felonious, very often harmfully self-delusional about all of the costs of war. They often confuse war with national security, while they use war to deconstruct the pillars of democratic laws protecting citizens internally, as hindrances to some phantom exogenous insecurity.

One of the worst recent jokes on humanity was the war to end all wars and all that followed, it did not, and it denigrated Germany, Hitler, leveled cities, and industries worldwide, it devolved three continents, the worst in human history. That was not the only one. Humanity often mistakes the static and momentary advantages of some small technological advancement, as cart blanch license to harm others interests and eventually others, the last millenniums' profound human errors are good examples.

While in dynamic time span, others learn and apply retaliatory technological advancements. Hence, the self-delusional tautological arguments, and the immense human and capital wasted resources, times, and lives continue.

Nations often lead headfirst and hope their initial technological injections will carry them through and cover all mistakes, collaterals, and tangible costs. The technological arbitrage between nation of Afghanistan and the old Soviet Union were the largest in resources and technological gap since the Vietnam War, which did not dissuade the results. Even without the westerns' technological injections, the resource-bleedings would have delivered both economies to the end of the mud hut fields. An unhappy solution, which Alexander and other Colonial kingdoms had found as an unpalatable defeatism. Civilized global plunderers of truth ought to reward Afghanis long suffering nation from their saviors from theological extremism, to modernity militarisms. Moreover, give that nation a few decades in real peace and prosperity to heal old national wounds, without the aid of opium's commerce to find and claw their way ought of the Dante's descriptive misfortunes. They live it, in real time.

The statements that modern wars cost $100-$200 million are dubious intellectual opiated misperceptions, too. Since, the most recent wars cost up to one trillion dollars. The actual Iraq War costs were 1-4 trillion dollars, which was supposedly to pay for itself. these are just a few examples. The war number games are dynamic and swiftly expand exponentially. They hide frauds of monumental proportions. In cases of even none legitimate defenses and national securities, the panicky responses are not to ask the hard questions first. Do we have a moral or ethical obligation to try diplomacy first? How we will pay for it? The beginning, the middle, and the after, collateral and veteran damages included, they all have costs. Do we stop bloodsheds, or do we actually add to them and prolong them. Where, why, what for, what we gain, what we lose, when and how long, why we are still there? And what we will accomplish, after the initial whole lots of nothings, the usual perpetual hate, and national and international resentments and animosities.

The pro-war crowd in USA, the Neocons, and neo-plutocrats, the international military-industrial and political complexes (the fifth column mobs) are the gerontocracy that will never admit those minor details are the bane of current $17 trillion deficit and global recession. They are looking around to expand their long war visions, to total religious wars, nuclear expansions, and forced conflicts over or under the tables, dismantling or fictionalizing the great American constitution and bill of rights, under the perpetual national security emergency conditions, bills of tenders, vanishing habeas corpus, evasive falsification of events, are also repetitious pattern stamps. Now it is the Islam-o-phobic rhetoric. Tomorrow, it will be something else. They have financially gained. The American middleclass had lost prominently and financially.[3] They have displaced, and devastated many people internationally.

These wars extended 9-11 logical defensive responses. However, now they are being perceived much differently as time has passed.[4] They are registering with the receiving nations as revenge excuses. They register now with Islamic nations much more hostile on them as nations and people, rather than delivering justice within the boundaries of the international order, ethics, or laws. Since, they have seen those laws violated repeatedly, in or out of the United Nation. They assume the war intends have long evolved into postcolonial retributions and humiliations, aiming at marginal states and nations that share the religion of Islam, and the worst of zeolites' wrath. This has induced the sickest intellectual zeolites, whom tend to pitch in, hiding behind freedom of speech or theology, to enflame, incite, or do worst in shadows of mobs and war psychoses globally.

They have declared hate-wars on multiculturalism in the west, war on Islamic faith in the East, and they spread ancient and new casus belli. Their false claims and vague generalities in its ignorance, all add to dangerous and different escalated-states of global insecurities. They also add to the heightened risks and uncertainties in domestic commerce. These make most nations more paranoid, and more prone to loose nuke minds, fearful preemptive wars and harmful actions, or pathological aimless muscular militarism, at the expense of constructive domestic economic activities. The 1995s, and 1960s gerontocracy do not deescalate, or add to constructive diplomatic solutions, toward peace, they have drained economic resources for other potentially positive solutions.

Any time confirmed serial sinners, can expand holy book burnings, or pornography making skills into international multi-continental killings and wars, we have devolved into new an unsustainable state of global diplomacy, which more wars will not cure.[5] This dangerous shift combined ultra-legal and self-imposed laws into transnational aggregations and aggressions can push allies into quiet victims, or passive aggressive combatants. Chronic post-colonial-hegemonic expansions against any nations are considered very hostile. These nations do not think they deserve it, nor have the American people mandated them. Most recent opinion polls have gone against recent wars by more than 51-65 percent. The mandates are on the other side of those pro war arguments.

Those constantly kicking us out there are neither allies, nor good functioning self-sustaining democratic models, nor any friend of United Nation. Israeli political rightwing radicals including, neocons and neoplutocratic media and gaming financial sources long ago decided to take a different inroads. They have firmly established themselves in the military-media-political and industrial complex arrangements. They apply counter pressures anytime their military and territorial expansive plans (not always to the national security advancements of United States) are in questions. The problem with their self-help strategies are that they involve Western interventionism into Islamic nations, at great political and financial costs, and collateral damages to the national security of United States, and all of these nations. That makes nations more hostile to Unites States.

These political and financial consequences the negative externalities of wars have mounted in trillions of dollars. This is despite the admonishment of President Dwight D. Eisenhower (1961), about mindless prolonged interventions, especially in the Middle East, beyond national security, which meant self-defense in cases of attacks on homelands. These economic activities, (like jobs-income-demand creation, infrastructures investments, and unlike preemptive and elective wars) are required for maintenance to sustain domestic economic wellbeing. These economic activities are required for circular flow to induce economic balance growth. They are essential for higher money velocity to allow demand for supply-side economics growth, dynamically.

The political democratic pressures in the Islamic countries are on a collision course with the hidden agendas and realities yet not disclosed to these nations population, neither by their own governments, and nor by Western cheering nations. Iran historical experiences with the anti-democratic pro-neo-plutocratic western politics and strategies of United States (like AJAC Operation against democratic prime minster of Iran, 1951) are vivid. These attitude and policies are contrary to the Western pro-freedom and pro-democracy speeches, and the documented promises of president Franklin D. Roosevelt of USA, Stalin of old Russia, and Churchill of UK, in the Tehran treaty.

These are historically detailed, and factual. They are inflamed with more recent history of war arrangement between USA, and Iraq, pre USA invasion of Iraq. Therefore, the Iranians have small and fleeting expectation that USA interests, in their lives and miseries are anything but exploitative for oil and other financial bases. They strongly suspect that the administrations cannot deliver on any conditional systematic agreements to scale back, or deescalate hostilities, even in a removal of economic sanctions on Iranian people, for abandonments of some future nuclear technological advancement in Iran. The only one chance left is a negotiated-grand bargain with compromise on all sides. Even though the global agreements are, for now, the current technological advancements are about the legal United Nation agreed nuclear energy programs of Iran. Because, the opposition party in united State have effectively stated, and then blocked progressive, corrective economic actions of the current administration, to the detriment of USA people, even inside USA. What chances will the long-suffering Iranian people have from the politicization of their legal programs?

The future fork in the road that scares USA oil-plutocrats, and pro-Israeli defense industry neo-plutocrats, American neocons is in the future. What has the Israeli radical-right in freight is a futuristic and imaginary real democracy in Iran, which will be able to defend Iranian territory and resources mainly oil, against neocon plutocratic expansionism, and the post neocolonial bulling and plunders, instead of international trade or commerce. All the same, different technological injections in natural gas development and technologies and electrical car technologies have made old logic for energy resources nihilistic needs and demands null. However, the politics on either side does not reflect the altered reality.

That is what the other side sees, behind the wizard of OZ curtain, under the tables, and in the dark back allies, of United Nation security arrangements. They are not against any international trade of their resources, oil included.

Unfortunately, the substantial consequences of these current exaggerated over-reactions have absolute dangerous contrary nihilistic day-after effects, which will push any Iranian government into their real nihilistic national security needs, versus the current energy needs.

The only present paradigm about nuclear Iran is, about their stated legal nuclear technology capabilities and energy demands. People whom are pushing wars, they are doing to plunder many people, the American middle class tax payers, and the Iranian economy, and the Palestinians independence aspirations, Arabians and African new democratic movements and their resources. They will find little cash rewards in these plundered coffers, after they have killed many innocent people, and engendered multigenerational enmities. Greater diplomats and intellectuals often avoid such mephitis mistakes. These evasive war dances of follies are a big disservice to history of Jewish scholars, whom would have consummated the fleeting opportunity of two state solutions and some peace with their own prime minster, whom their extremists murdered, three presidents ago.

The worst consequences of current lunacy, and economic pressures, and militarily aggressive gestures in the Persian Gulf, and any actual attacks by Israeli, or their proxies, in illegal transgressions, are the legitimizations of third world countries to engage in preemptive nuclear developments, nuclear proliferations, arrangement to access nuclear resources (even by NGTs). These nihilistic aggressive and non-diplomatic destabilizations cultivate retaliations, revenge attacks, after further illegal acts. These are formulas for permanent destabilization. These marches of follies tend to delegitimize the United Nations purpose and charter. At this time, those resources can be properly used to get food to all hungry mouths, internationally, and improve ever so stingily the human squalid conditions, against global drought, extreme weather alterations, unskilled youth, and population growth. As the technological advancement enables us to improve level of global lives, all of these empty war drums on international scene are disgustingly embracing display of hooliganism, not cultural enlightenments, despite the shameless spins. More thoughtful resource managements are required.

That is not the worst of it. They have already encouraged, and they will further motivate NGTs. What is worst, it is opening opportunities for nongovernmental actors to use their usual tactics, use massive conventional anti-ship attacks, or even nuclear level attacks, if they get their hands on them, and hide behind nations engaged in hot aimless rhetorical conflicts. The kind of destructive show boating, we see these days, pastors burning holy books, criminals denigrating religious icons, are further manifestation of these psychotic terroristic tendencies. They are the other shoes that are flanged around, sometimes in advanced, educated, developed nations. What should we expect from the enflamed, humiliated, insulted, uneducated, educated unemployed and hopeless hungry masses?

We blame the moderate of these nations for felonious reasons, with criminal intend to do harm, to win cheap political points, or theological political chess moves. These do not advance civility, modernity, civilizations, or improve human conditions, and they do a disservice to true theological worshipers globally. The diplomacy could have pushed an agenda of Gandhi, Dr. King, Mandela, or educational economic development and growth, instead of these expansive-aimless militarisms. We are well educating them in the wrong skills, and mortified when they use the militaristic skills we thought them.

Those are other reasons to dissuade the Israeli political radicals and Western national neo-plutocrats to deescalate conflicts, rather than monetize regional conflicts to hide their resource striping and land-grab strategies, beside the global drug lords trades, or other criminal activities, and money grabbing intends. This is the worst economic example of Keynesian beg thy neighbor policy. It has morphed into, destroy, bully, and plunder your neighbors, in the post-war psychosis period. The results have been consequential for western economies, and any advancement of humanitarian growth and development economic strategies. Israeli president Peres in Doha, Qatar recently said, the reasons of Gandhi, Dr. King, and President Mandela are much more persuasive fruitful paths for the youth, than the suicides-bleeders on the global scenes, these include the Israelis young soldiers, too. Many young men of the region have grown old, looking for the promised fruits of peace and modernity. However, the orchards have been confiscated, the old trees have been up-rooted, the new trees have not been planted, they cannot see, or plant trees for themselves. Therefore, they think you cannot deliver. Everyone has a choice to deescalate, and rethink constructively, anew.

The endgames have constantly gone against initial mostly fabricated, frequently exaggerated wordy game-intends, or results. The depressed global economies and hordes of jobless populations are also victims, of these nonsensical militarisms.[6] These are also adding to the dangerous dynamics, which the self-leaking ice cream and military profiteering will encompass. The results will not be to spread functional democracy and free market progress, it will shut down that progress, too.[7] The proof is the last twenty years of elective wars, and the deteriorating level of lives and human conditions. The same conditions which these wars were to improve; however, some economic models show glimmers of hopes they may actually improve.

EXAMPLES OF HARMFUL VERBALISM

The pathological needs of the neocons and dangerous terroristic outside-forces (NGTs) for any total-long wars, or a war on Islam, have mushroomed again 2012. It is usual, given the times and circumstances of waning failing wars, the spins have been cultivated. There is more than greed behind them. It is the result of desperate failing grasps, after many years of failing their other masters, rather than American constitution, American patriotic duties, American economy, even industrial, and global economies, after using and abusing religious idols and theological falsehoods. Some of their arguments are dishonestly constructed, ignorantly concocted, and criminally enacted.

They have to conjure wars, enemies, peculiar victimization scenarios with bewailing, lamentations and blubber, while they are busy inflicting brutal Hitlerism, and label racisms on their victimized neighbors, passerby civilians, x-presidents and concerned politicians, student of human conditions, and tribes in their own homes, lands, and orchards. Islam and radicalism are new petticoats to cover it, American friendship and politics, media links, and the United Nation are new burkas and vales to hide their serial violations of the United Nation's charters, and ending multiple American bipartisan presidential mandates for the two state Israeli-Palestinian solutions. These are the mendacity of their political lamentations; however, the wailers are self-bleeders of modern economies. While with the same breath they denigrate the same institutions, they want them to declare long-wars on Islam, but this country first, that country next. They also have ended the mandates. Just give us the taxpayer cash, let us steal land,

and destroy the landowners, when they object. Do away with your civilian control of military, let us bewail and lament the new casus belli, but activate military courts inland, strike down that habeas corpus, and fictionalize those annoying constitutional checks and balances, no transparencies for you citizen noisemakers, and voters. Darn those constitutionally required citizen-petitions. Let the backward states erase the citizen-petitions off the legal books. Why even bother with the national elections? Otherwise, do not be too inquisitive, or we will put our own people in your offices. Real allies ought to know, how Americans perceive them, while a few misguided politicians emulate them, and encourage their misguidances.

These nonsenses from the failed-neocons are only the gloves, the steal hands of radical political party from Israeli military have chosen them, for their orphisms, they have lingered and imposed on American politics for 12 to

13 years.[8] They only expose themselves one limb at time, not unlike their mimickers in the original radical Sunni Wahhabis Muslims, and the Al-Qaida that they unhinged, far from all of Sunni Wahhabis, or all of Islam, which they now want to ridicule and blame, in their ignorance they may have unhinged more groups. They have to push an agenda of war to occupy political space. The only good advice to others is, do not overreact to their overt hate mongering, their pointed wars' dictates, and their moral and ethical ambiguities. Humanities depleting resources will not afford prolonged wasteful militarism, after last millennial failed models.

They have ignored and trashed the United Nation's charters, USA presidential mandates, and humanitarian red lines for many years.[9] They, the neocons overt attacks have been not only on an embassy, but in multiple attacks on the office of presidency in perceived vulnerable times.[10] When an ambassador and servants of American people are fallen, even without condolences to the fallen families, all the while they have been constantly instigating, warmongering, abstracting, and obstructing all economic and political constructive-moves.[11] They scream at the Americans that they are allies and democracies.[12] They turn loose their agents' provocateurs in purchased and planted media enshrine torture-laws and shark the shallows of American academia to silence scholars readily, to tag anti-Semitic charges profusely from student to professors to presidents.[13] It is provocatively, the most demonstratively discoursing exhibitionisms of thoughtless un-democracy possible.[14] Every well-read polemicist in politics that lacks arithmetic knowledge uses Machiavelli to push fear over diplomacy.[15] That is a very perverse Euro-Colonial idea of obtrusive abuse of American constitutional democracy, and American public servants of any or no denominations.

They have killed scientists, their own prime minster, and diplomats before. They are just expanding their uncivilized fuliginous war psychoses wider. Nevertheless, they failed miserably, and bankrupted the American and global economies failing miserably, already. Therefore, they rely on emotionalism, ignorance, anger, war mongering, and their new mantra, Islam-o-phobia and the post war psychosis.[16] However, their ultimate weapon is their hope for overreactions to their hate speeches, one to set off the uneducated mobs aflame with America as an enemy of Islam despite many American presidents' statements, second to push dangerous automaton empty-vessels on American-voters.[17] Neither, of those choices is winning any hearts or minds, their constituencies ought to replace them with better logical constructs. The latter has had the most depletive consequential results for American economy and global democracy movements.

The one two punches we have seen before, no matter how much they deny it now, it reappear slyly again.[18] That is how the constitution has been fictionalized, using slow boiling the frog strategies, against the public repeated mandate against unconstitutional misconducts and endless wars.[19] Of course, their first options are that they be in the key military and decision positions, if they can fool enough voters.[20] That is up to the American-Voters, not them and their masters, in finance, in media, in gaming, or in foreign nations.

That is why, it is important to see those ten-year taxes, and the real persons (not corporate) depositors in those offshore bank accounts, at least, for the office of the presidency.[21] American people may have to widen those official requirements for all major political offices, even at state levels. Benjamin Franklin said about security and liberty still holds, once you give up liberty to bargain for some security, soon you will have neither. To rephrase old Ben, once you barging liberty for some democracy, soon you have no liberty, either.

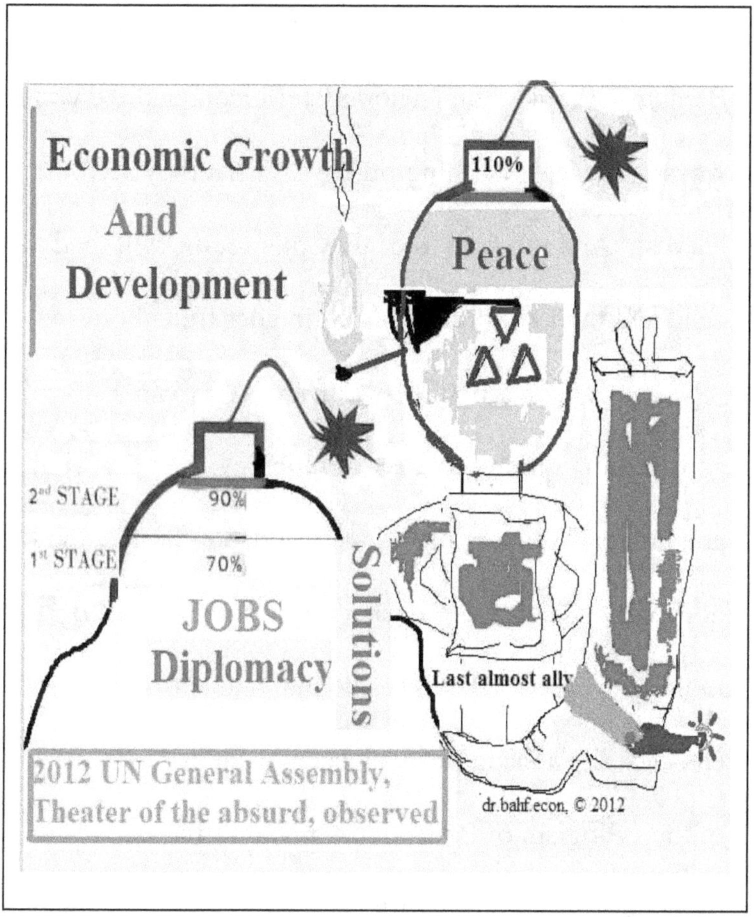

The neocons have now united, except that the extremism they have cultivated in Middle East and elsewhere are their own hate puppets as well, we just do not wish they succeeded in imposing one in the White House and on The American-voters, unannounced.[22] The voters already learned from scientific experimentalisms of Benjamin Franklin and Thomas Jefferson, and the winning ways of George Washington days, "what they seed they harvest. And the fruit trees they plant now, will feed the aged and their children, bearing fresher fruits."

There are good lessons from American constitutional representative democracy.[23] Bill of rights and numerous amendments were added to perfect the living document. There have been a lot of poor starts and stops. In the November 2012, presidential and national American election, the neocons will succeed or fail to disprove some of the syllogism of President Abraham Lincoln's hypothesis, at the substantial cooperate financed election. Hypothesis 1, it is possible to fool most of the American people most of the time, using all of the expanded powers and technologies injections afforded by the Teconomic of verbalism and cooperate finance. Hypothesis 2, it is not possible, to fool most of the people most of the time, regardless of the money spent, and technological injections of verbalism employed. At least for now, we can reject hypothesis 1, and accept hypothesis 2.[24] That is, one of President Abraham Lincoln's idioms still holds in the America. That ought to be good for the democracy.

NOTES

[1] Dr. Bahman Fakhraie advances new research in this field. His upcoming book title is, Political *Teconometrics*, 2013?.

[2] These laws in democracies allow functionality without patronage, peonage, slavery, and obligatory services, for perpetual (dynamic) system functionality. These supplement Adam smith profit motivation, by livable wages, and dynamic survival of the system, an important point of contention, and an issue with classic economic orthodoxy. The holistic unorthodoxy here resolves those dynamic issues.

[3] Norman Finkelstein, *"Knowing Too Much: Why the American Jewish Romance With Israel is Coming to an End,* Amazon.com,
http://www.orbooks.com/catalog/knowing-too-much/

[4] Tutu Says Bush and Blair Should Face Court Over Iraq. Archbishop Desmond M. Tutu wrote that the two former leaders should be made to "answer for their actions" in the 2003 invasion of Iraq., www.nytimes.com,October 13 at 8:59pm
http://www.nytimes.com/2012/09/03/world/europe/tutu-says-bush-and-blair-should-face-court-over-iraq.html?_r=2&

[5] Education and comprehension are good for everyone.
1-http://www.youtube.com/watch?v=oeIfj5hJsh0
2-http://vimeo.com/29349773,

[6] "People want jobs and the prospect of a decent life. All too often, what they get instead is divisiveness… delay... and denial of their dreams and aspirations," read the rest of the speech at the following link, http://www.un.org/apps/news/infocus/sgspeeches/statments_full.asp?statID=1660#Secretary-General Ban Ki-moon, General Assembly, 25 September 2012.

[7] The neo-plutocracy reduced demand for domestic workers by estimated 30 percent in United States, because, they outsourced and replaced them by technologies, or even cheaper, less regulated international workers in hinterlands. All the while, they were pushing supply side job creation mantras, and trickle-down hocus-pocus, they were exporting lower level of living standards, and harsh conditions, none union theologies abroad. That is not free trade, and free market utopic expansionism, it is profiteering and lower level of living dystopia.

[8] John J. Mearsheimer and Stephen M. Walt, "The Israeli

Lobby and U.S. Foreign Policy"

[9] http://www.orbooks.com/catalog/knowing-too-much/ http://www.nytimes.com/2007/06/11/arts/11depa.html Outspoken Political Scientist Denied Tenure at DePaul, http://www.economist.com/node/21556892/print, Peter Beinart, "The Crisis of Zionism,"

[10] Steve Benen, Obama will be able to lose Kansas, fair and square, *MSNBC*, Mon Sep 17, 2012 1:19 PM EDT,

http://maddowblog.msnbc.com/_news/2012/09/17/13918204-obama-will-be-able-to-lose-kansas-fair-and-square?lite

[11] Barak Ravid, Netanyahu launches unprecedented attack on U.S. government, on 9-11;*Reuters and The Associated Press*, 13:34 11.09.12, 78

[12] Prime Minister Benjamin Netanyahu on Tuesday launched an unprecedented verbal attack on the U.S. government over its stance on the Iranian nuclear program. http://www.haaretz.com/news/middle-east/netanyahu-those-that-refuse-to-set-red-lines-for-iran-can-t-give-israel-red-light.premium-1.464278

[13] Marjorie Cohn, *A Legal Duty to Prosecute Torturers*, JURIST - Forum, Oct. 1, 2012, http://jurist.org/forum/2012/10/marjorie-cohn-torture-prosecution.php

[14] Outspoken Political Scientist Denied Tenure at DePaul. http://www.nytimes.com/2007/06/11/arts/11depa.html.
An older Persian wisdom, "Read a lot, and say little, and only if it helps."
John J. Mearsheimer and Stephen M. Walt, "The Israeli Lobby and U.S. Foreign Policy"
Norman Finkelstein, *"Knowing Too Much: Why the American Jewish Romance With Israel is Coming to an End, " 472* from Amazon.com,
http://www.orbooks.com/catalog/knowing-too-much/,
http://www.economist.com/node/21556892/print
Peter Beinart, “The Crisis of Zionism,”

[15] Niall Ferguson, Obama's Mideast Meltdown: The president fiddles as the world burns, *The daily beast*, September 17, 2012

[16] Most likely an Al-Qaeda attack, became a dangerous political football? However, the timeline suggest premeditative political arrangements, which deduces sadder scenarios of ineptitudes, or mischiefs among them.
Michael O'Brien and Catherine Chomiak, Timeline: Political fallout from the attack on diplomats in Libya, *NBCNews.com,* September 17, 2012, 8:37, http://firstread.nbcnews.com/_news/2012/09/12/13831714-timeline-political-fallout-from-the-attack-on-diplomats-in-libya

[17] These political one-two steps, we have seen after 9-11. Sadly, this scenario has worked very badly on American body politics, which have now embedded 9-11 reactionary politics and multiple wars, in their radical right domestic politics.
Peter Beinart, "Bibi thinks he can push the U.S. around. Think again." *The Daily Beast,* September 17, 2012 1:00 AM EDT
http://www.thedailybeast.com/newsweek/2012/09/16/peter-beinart-on-netanyahu-s-bullying-act.print.html

[18] Prime Minister Benjamin Netanyahu on Tuesday launched an unprecedented verbal attack on the U.S. government over its stance on the Iranian nuclear program. http://www.haaretz.com/news/middle-east/netanyahu-those-that-refuse-to-set-red-lines-for-iran-can-t-give-israel-red-light.premium-1.464278

[19] Joe Palazzolo, Life after the War with Al Qaeda, *The Wall Street journal*, November 30, 2012, 12:58 PM ET, http://blogs.wsj.com/law/2012/11/30/pentagon-lawyer-describes-life-after-the-war-with-al-qaeda/

[20] It is an opinion, that too often, long wars are misused to cover the sins of almost allies, that only complicates and compounds the losses, unfortunately. About those sadder political scenarios, it is true that some Israeli foreign leader, an American presidential candidate, and the other Neocons quickly reappeared to capitalize on the shocked administration, on political scene Tuesday and Wednesday, even before any knowledge of the Libyan embassy was out. Once more, was this only coincidence, or a mistake, again? There are very few recurring coincidences in politics this raw, from such proactive-deluded masters of universe with history of overreach and misconducts? The multiple assumptive deductive hypotheses of the cabal thesis pass beyond the dismissive stages of conspiracy, very unwelcoming from almost allies and cohorts.
David Remnick, Neocon Gambits, *The New Yorker*, September 12,2012, http://www.newyorker.com/online/blogs/newsdesk/2012/09/have-benjamin-netanyahus-attacks-on-obama-gone-too-far.html?printable=true&currentPage=all

[21] The moment when Romney lost,

http://maddowblog.msnbc.com/_news/2012/10/17/14507198-the-moment-when-romney-lost
maddowblog.msnbc.com

[22] Maureen Dowd, Neocons Slither Back, *New York Times,* September 15, 2012 http://www.nytimes.com/2012/09/16/opinion/sunday/dowd-neocons-slither-back.html?src=me&ref=general

[23] For more detailed economic foundations you can read: Dr. Bahman Fakhraie, *TECONOMIC ANALYSIS, ANALYTICAL ECONOMIC REMEDIES FOR THE POST-CRASH MILLENNIAL ECONOMIES*, Utah FERDAT Publishing, 2012

[24] More than 2 billion dollars each spent on each election 2012, excluding the now legal outside cooperation.

CHAPTER 3

DATA ANALYSIS OF STATE CARFT OF VERBALISM

Nevertheless, the value theory of the aggregated data points out the imperfections of political market places inflect forces on lawmakers in the political markets and the mega finance market makers, active in the economic markets.[1] However, both entities faint ignorance of their documented deeds. In our modern case studies, these new concepts are more developed in this other recent book.[2]

Figure 5 shows Elasticity of rate of growth for selected variable per 1 percent growth of GDP.[3] That is, for 1 percent in increase in GDP, only 1 percent is spend on investment growth, 2 percent on consumers' growth rates, in addition, an unsustainable 3 percent are spent on a defense related and none domestic investments growth rates and endeavors.

In discussion of deficit and governmental expenditures, facts take misshapen detours. While domestic private investment has remained the same, personal disposable income per capital and private consumer expenditures have been flattened, national defense industrial complexes have increased since 1980s. Therefore, imperfections of either markets or both have developed in catastrophic financial consequences at the aggregated data level for the national economy, which are far beyond the capabilities of monetary normal functions

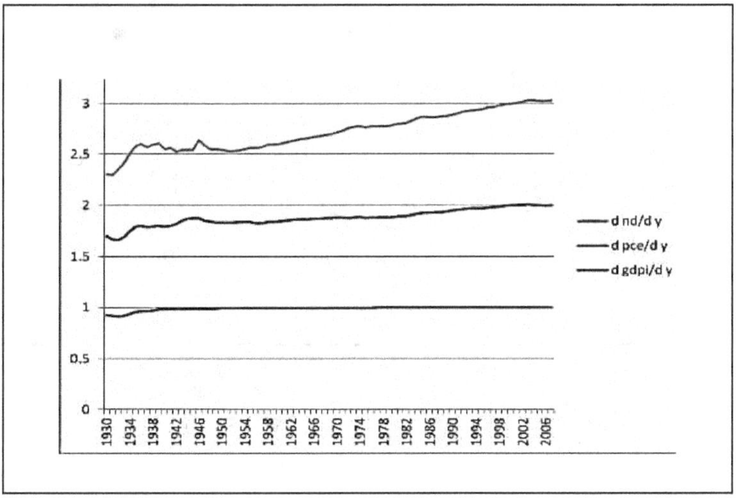

Figure 5, Elasticity of rate of growth of variables &GDP.

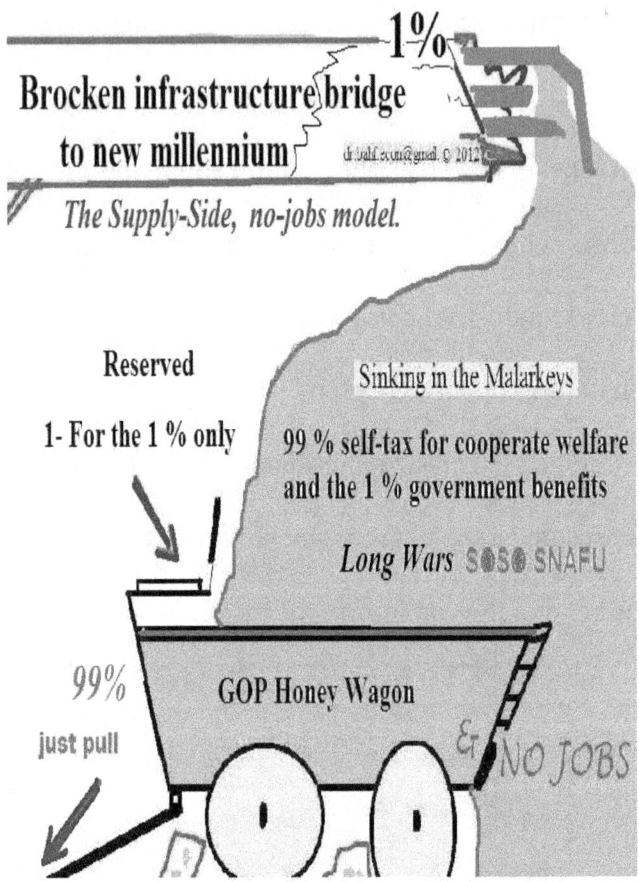

The broken tinkle-down economic model.

VERBALISM AND AMERICAN WORKERS

American Workers have entertained many words against them, while the interest income shares, and profit revenues have piled up elsewhere, in the upper income brackets. Even to the detriment of demand side of the anemic post-recession economies, the lopsided wealth concentration, disproportionate progressive tax breaks (legal or otherwise) have continued. The stubborn facts of dynamic aggregated data have not dissuaded but the rarest of the few enlighten mega billionaires. One has to understand that theoretically, from the 24 hours' time limit, only approximately 8 hours are used coherently and fully functional at work. The reduction in rest and 8 hours of sleep is also linked increasingly with reduce productivity and unconstructive efficiency, like in drowsy driving. The underpayments of workers have forced many contrary arrangements. While the labor market complexities are more evolved, the blood and toil union earned 8/8/8 formula for sleep, work, and living have been challenged by computerized-robotics-industrialization, unattested at great private costs to individuals budgets, and aggregated data through demand constraints, governmental revenue shortfalls and government services.[4] They will add up to the costs in the eventual cost and benefit analysis of different communities.

The vanished hours from familial duties, assistances to children education at home, or health maintenance related attendances influence work performances.[5] Thus, negotiated higher salaries of workers, shareholders returns on equities, or higher-incomes tax-rates, and more services by government were waved off for higher profits, higher bonuses, and executive salaries of smaller group of elites.[6] The political media spin behind this consequential elitism blames the educators' unions. While their stratagem is to bleed the educational arrangements, which retrains employees and put out global graduates, whom the private

The fine art and science of losing constituencies and elections, with the middle class and immigrants.

industries do not wish to employ, in favor of wealth concentration rather than wealth creation. The vanished hours or pays from employees for education and retraining for new employments are taken out of the savings of those human capitals as well.[7] Thus, negotiated higher salaries by unions, or higher taxes and transfers and services by government can balance out the negative savings in aggregate data of the economy.

The vanished countercyclical capacities of government-employment (tax and employment) will make revisiting the depression more probable. When the economy is in real trouble, like a depression, there never is any money to collect. Those are some of many good reasons President Franklin D. Roosevelt adopted these counter cyclical strategies, after many years of brutal political battles against republicans, Supreme Court, and business interests and the lobbies of wealth concentrations, instead of wealth creation by jobs, and wealth building interests.

The damnation of the golden-calf worshipers in this realm are not in their theological confusion for payments, but it is their malfeasance in abandonments of their offices, as servants of people and their good ethical senses for fees, lobbyist payola, and getting caught doing it. That intellectual malfeasance is the point of this academic admonition. Their religions will deal with their sinning methodologies, which are not the focus of any scientific expeditions, especially in this paper. Even thou, in their religion their sins and their impurities of motives, often were proven terminal with burning or drowning, a few generations back in the inquisition era.

This inquisition is an inquiry with scientific methodology and deductive reasoning to use voluminous addition of used words, constructively in order to improve level of living and human conditions globally, not by overreactions and mob scenes, but by mere presence of better ideas, and progressive scientific constructionism.

Flextime work accommodation has a lot of merit, however, the union standards and life quality presentation ought not to be vanished in competition with jailhouse, slaved, neo-peonage, and political prisoner workers of the American posterities, or hinterlands.[8] Those are also imperfections injected into the work market place.[9] That is an imperfect (perverted) version of market-capitalism, but it not the perfect-market-capitalism. The unpleasant consequences show in terms of lower GDP, higher poverty rates, lower life expectancies are important.

Despite the recent love affair of Wall Street financiers with neo-management techniques, profit only ledgers, or executive pay packages, or multimillion dollars new market offers, these do not justify the damages to the aggregated data, dynamic sustainable growth, stable job markets, and balanced dynamic income growth, and the overall economy. They are important injections, huge injection of wealth in individual finances (the 1 percent), and great limiting impacts in aggregate data.

However, they do not make for 3-6 percent GDP growth for decades, the kinds that sustained USA economy in 1940s, 50s economies. The kinds of technological injections, which have had multi-generational and sustained up lifting affects in lives of all people, and the most expansive dynamic growth in American middle class, that great none jingoistic exceptionalsim that mattered, and can matter again.

The reduced level of living and the decline in the real disposable income of workers (not in the median incomes) will influences supply shifts as well. That is not a global constructive competition for sustainable markets, economic growth, or economic development. That is a race to the bottom by profiteering, which will drug constructive economies further from free enterprise democratic solution for unsustainable uncreative destructions.

This is a hedge fund mangers' psychosis and potentially anti-social maneuvering around accommodating legal institutions, thwacked by the same financiers, and their handpicked political servants, taking advantages of democratic free-market principles to act without moral or ethical business codes, social consciences, or political principles.[10] Schumpeter explained micro economic odd events, terminating decision points, obsolete production processes.

These same principles applied at aggregate levels, with the aid of super technological expediencies, make for the same effect the looters and plunders of old British villages had on those small economies, at much larger scales.

In modern economies, we need to multiply those with billion and trillions of dollars to realize the potencies of miss applied creative destructions, without technological injections and creative constructions against cyclical shocks. This are badly needed because of losses in government jobs to sustain economies, which are experiencing (this millennial structural-unemployment) upward of 30 percent drop in their base employment industries.[11]

Whence will these reparative mega capital injection or technological injections come to save the vulnerable modern economies from the marauders, the looters on their white horses and fake capitalists' white night armors?[12] There is only one answer to this 30-year conundrum.

Therefore, the misapplications of Schumpeterian creative destruction concept, combined with the penchants of under payment or nonpayment of taxes, which need to match the heightened technologically-enhanced level of social harm and negative economic externalities, to repair societies damages of these techniques are devastating.

The proof, the evidentiary results in unemployment, underemployment of resources and inputs, pollutions, and termination of many production processes, the proofs are hiding in plain sights.

MONETARISM AND THE VELOCITY OF MONEY

The definition of velocity of money is nominal GDP divided by a measure of the money supply. It is defined as the rate of turnover in the money supply. That is, the number of times one dollar in hands of different consumers is used to purchase final goods and services included in that GDP of the same economy.

The income elasticity of money supply is introduced here for the first time to assist student and scholar of monetarism in their fields of study, for this period. It studies the growth of each dollar of GDP per each dollar of money supply injected in the economy.

Nominal GDP is defined as the Gross domestic product (GDP), the featured measure of U.S. output, is the market value of the all goods and services produced by labor and property (human and tangible capital, skilled workers) located in the United States in current dollars denominations. In this example the quarterly measurement of this money supply index.

M1, index of money supply includes funds that are readily accessible for spending as cash, and convertible to cash transactions. M1 consists of:

- Currency outside the U.S. Treasury, Federal Reserve Banks, and the vaults of depository institutions;
- Traveler's checks of nonbank issuers;
- Demand deposits;
- Other checkable deposits (OCDs), which consist primarily of negotiable order of withdrawal (NOW) accounts at depository institutions and credit union share draft accounts.

Seasonally adjusted M1 is the sum of currency, traveler's checks, demand deposits, and OCDs, each seasonally adjusted separately. The measurements used in this teconomic studies are estimated quarterly.

MZM, Money Zero Maturity index of money supply include M2 less small-denomination time deposits plus institutional money funds.[13] In this example the quarterly measurement of this money supply index.

Real Gross Domestic Product, with 1 Decimal (GDPC1), is calculated in billions of Chained 2005 Dollars, Quarterly, Seasonally Adjusted Annual Rate.[14] Nominal Gross Domestic Product, with 1 Decimal (GDP), is calculated in billions of Dollars, Quarterly, Seasonally Adjusted Annual Rate.[15] Rates of growth and decay of gross domestic products are calculated by author, using natural logarithm of the indices.

In this study, velocity of money is a ratio of nominal GDP to a measure of the money supply, M1, or

MZM for the same period. It can be thought of as the rate of turnover in the money supply in the transactional economy. That is, the number of times one dollar is used to purchase final goods and services included in the nominal gross national product, GDP.

The next two figures show that despite the increase in money supply shown by higher money velocity picks (in figure 6), the rate of change in GDP is reduced, that is the multiple troughs shown (in figure 7), for the decade of 2000.

Figure 6 shows money velocities for M1 and MZM, in United States.

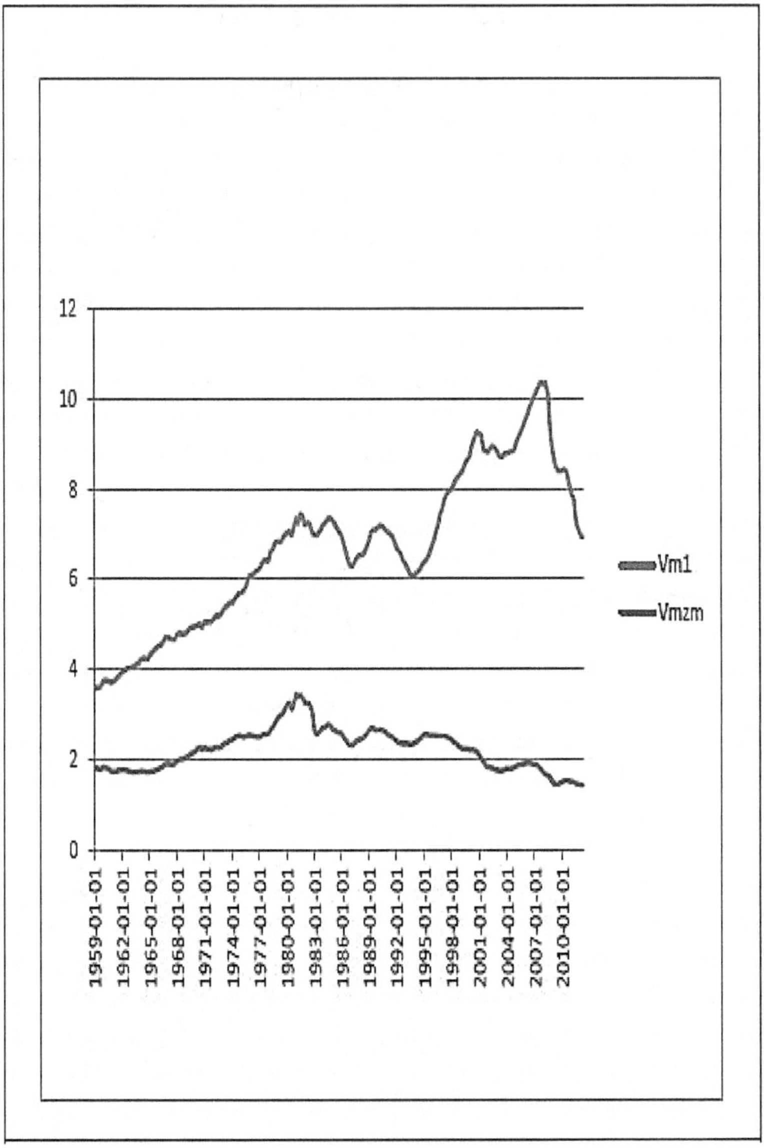

Figure 6, Money velocity for USA, quarterly 1959-2009.

The M1 shows transactional characteristic. That is, its turnover in the economy is more frequent and larger than MZM index, which has more of saving characteristic.

Figure 7 shows income elasticity of money supplies of both (M1, MZM, quarterly 1950-2009) in United States.

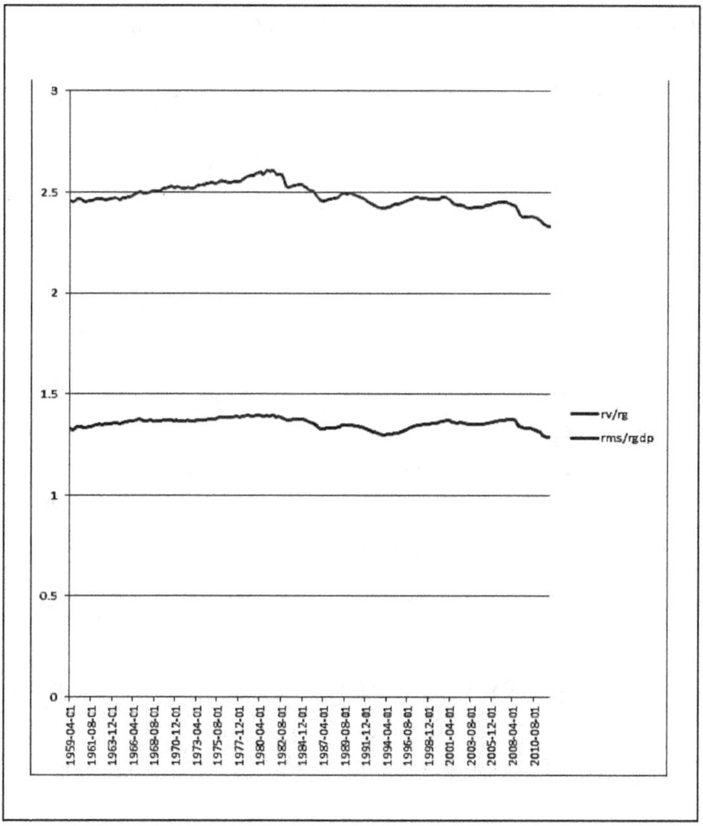

Figure 7, Income elasticity of money USA q.1959-2009.

Despite the transactional nature of M1, and saving natural tendencies of MZM, the income elasticity of M1 and MZM are remarkably reflective of each other, while latter has a bigger impact by about more than one percentage point. One of the implications, reflecting the lower curve, is the depletion of national saving, as well as individual depletion of savings, influencing the last down trend in the economy. In simpler words, people were running out of transactional money after their savings were depleted in recent recession.

The analytical academic interpretations of this new research have significant policy implications for United States Federal Reserves, and Central Banks internationally. It shows the rates of growth or decay for each additional dollars of money supply added to the economy, measured by GDP growth.

Figure 8 shows the current nominal, chained (real) gross domestic product of USA.

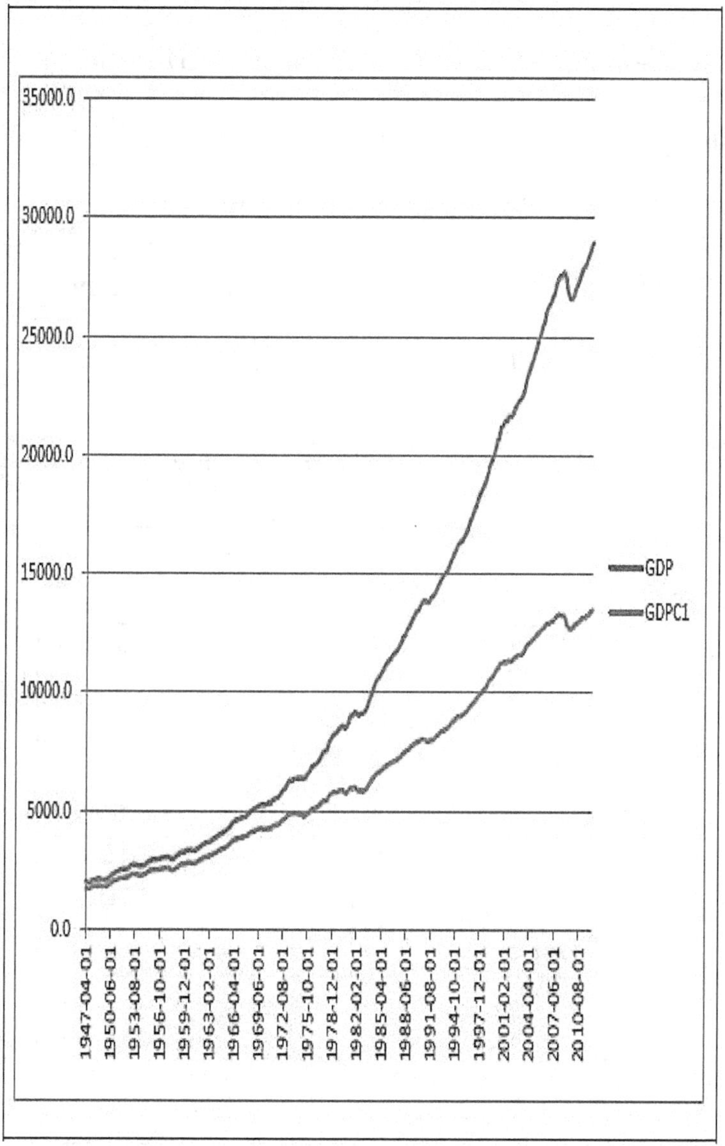

Figure 8, GDP, and GDPC1 for USA quarterly 1947-2009.

All US Government employees are in thousands of persons, monthly data, seasonally adjusted. Total Private Industry's employees are in thousands of persons, in monthly data, seasonally adjusted.

Figure 9 shows us the graphs of these monthly employment measurements in the economy.

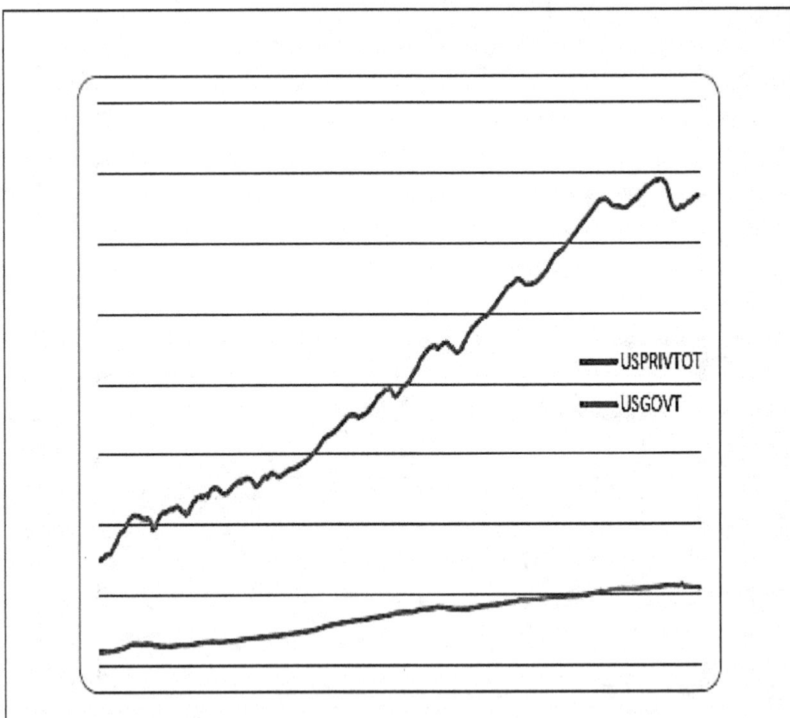

Figure 9, P. & G. employment, USA data for 1939-2009.

It is important to understand the amount of income or funds that are active in the economy, and are measured in GDP as economic activities, since they formulated the aggregate demand in the economy.

The economically significant points are deduced from the initial increasing slope of private employment, which flattens in 2000s, and the flatter slopes of government employment, since 1990s. Another important and compounding influence developed during late 1990s. The slope of private employment curve has flattened significantly since that time.[16] That is structurally shows in the recent unemployment data.

Figure 10 studies the private and government wages and private income on assets. The impacts of these combined influences are reflected throughout the economy.[17] Wages denotes employees' wages. Government pays the wages in (wages_gov).

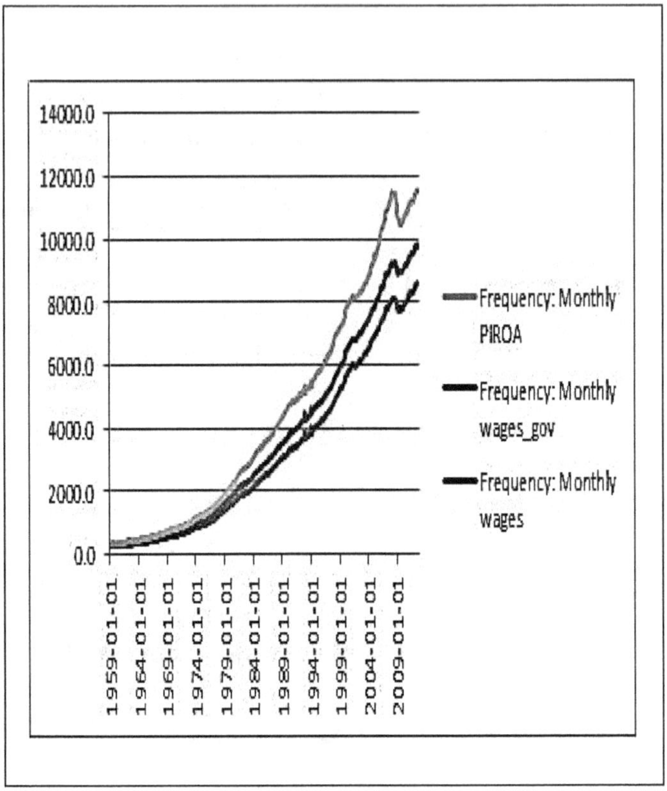

Figure 10, P & G wages, private assets' income.

Personal Income Receipts on Assets data is in billions of dollars, monthly, seasonally adjusted at an annual rate. In this study, implications are shown in income and revenues, and finally as private consumption. Figure 11 shows private industry wages and salaries, disposable income, and consumption in USA economy. Because, USA income, wages, salaries, and personal return on assets, and disposable personal income are related to the economic activity (aggregate demand side) and GDP. The important changes have been that since 1970s, the private interest income has surpassed the wage and salary components in aggregated data.

Figure 11 shows wages and salaries in current dollars for private industry, the private disposable income, and private consumption expenditures in the United States, since 1959. While the current wages and disposable personal income have increased the private consumption expenditures data has not. The current dollar aggregated data is use here to show all measurements have increase. Those indicating the private industry wages and salaries, and those indicating the disposable personal income per capita have dynamically increased.

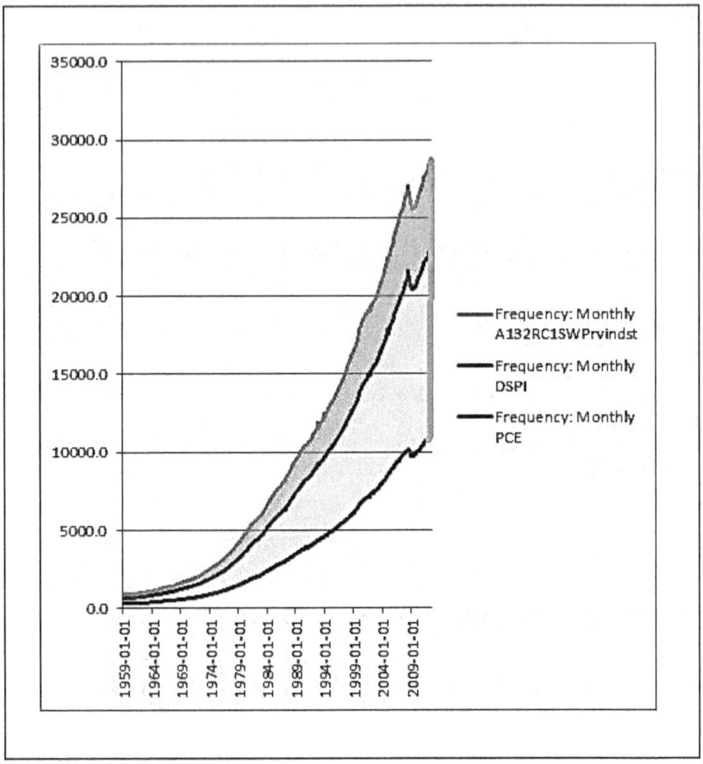

Figure 11, P. wages, D. income, and consumption.

However, the gaps between those two measurements and the one measuring current private consumptions expenditures have also increased over time. The same explanation can assist us in comprehension of another modern conundrum, which is presented in figure 12. Figure 12 shows the gap between current USA tax revenues and transfer payments.

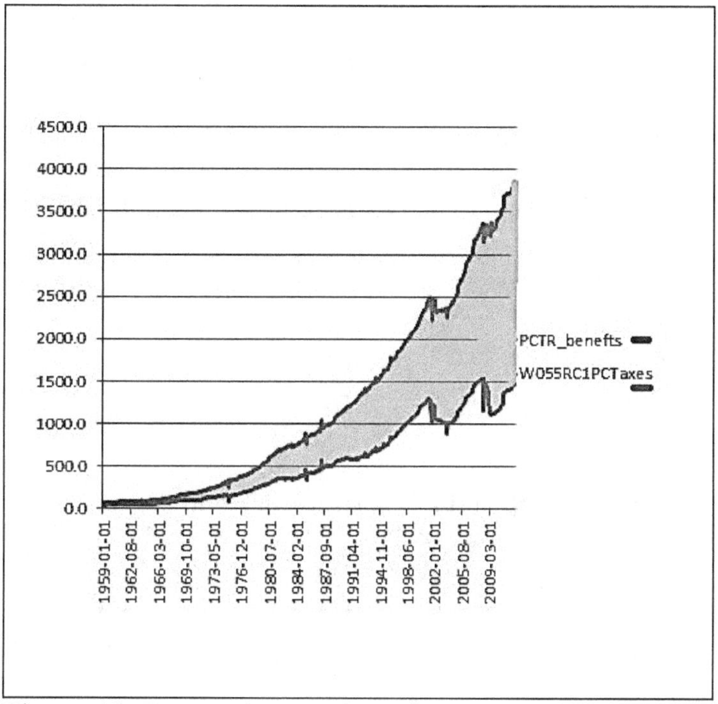

Figure 12, Personal taxes, benefits, USA 1959- 2009.

Data shows graphically that late 1990s alterations to the laws projected the major influences on the economy, including the double dip downturns in the global financial markets and international economy.

Therefore, the flatting of private employment curve (figure 9), tax law changes impacting government revenues from assets incomes (figure 10), and number of dependents shown as the increased gap in current disposable personal income (figure 11) influenced, and increased the benefit deficits in (figure 12).

The syllogisms explored have been the bases of polemicists' presentations about policy and economic policies for the last few decades.

Here are a few correct ones:

- Wealth and income concentrations are towards higher assets
- Private and government employment levels show divergence
- Policy miss-applications has been targeted
- Tax rate adjustment and tax burden have transferred to payroll incomes.
- High-income asset tax returns dropped by 50 percent.
- Elasticity of added money supply decreasingly adds to GDP growth.

- Motivational blocks to corrections of policy errors, or deliberate inactions.
- Consequential economic downturns and multiple dipping are noted.
- There are known divergences, between high income tax break and employment

It is important to realize how consequentialists are pushing false remedy of only tax break for the cooperate sector, which now under "citizen law," can purchase their own government out of the greatest dysfunctional democracy.

There is very little than irrationality of verbigeration defending indefensible positions for accumulated wealth, rather than the processes of income generations, which are the only economic method that can create jobs.

Private property protections, is understandable, job securities, retaining, education to job tracks, laws to encourage domestic investments, are rational processes.

Unfortunately, none of those processes for wealth creations was noted, defended, or protected, so profusely for so long, the focus was and remained wealth concentration. They were and have not been mutually exclusive concepts in science of economic, but in the art of political statecraft.

However, they succumbed to the art of political lobbying. On the false assertions that money or wealth alone creates jobs, wealthy people were as much in the dark after the 1929 crash in United States, and for some decades, after that period.

All of their forceful assertions and paroxysmal laws added to the depression harms. Simply the risks were so high that wealth-concentrators flee the economy, even some risk-averse governments and presidents were unable to apply statecraft fully.

Figure 13 shows the growth and decay rates of real GDP, USA 1959 to 2012.

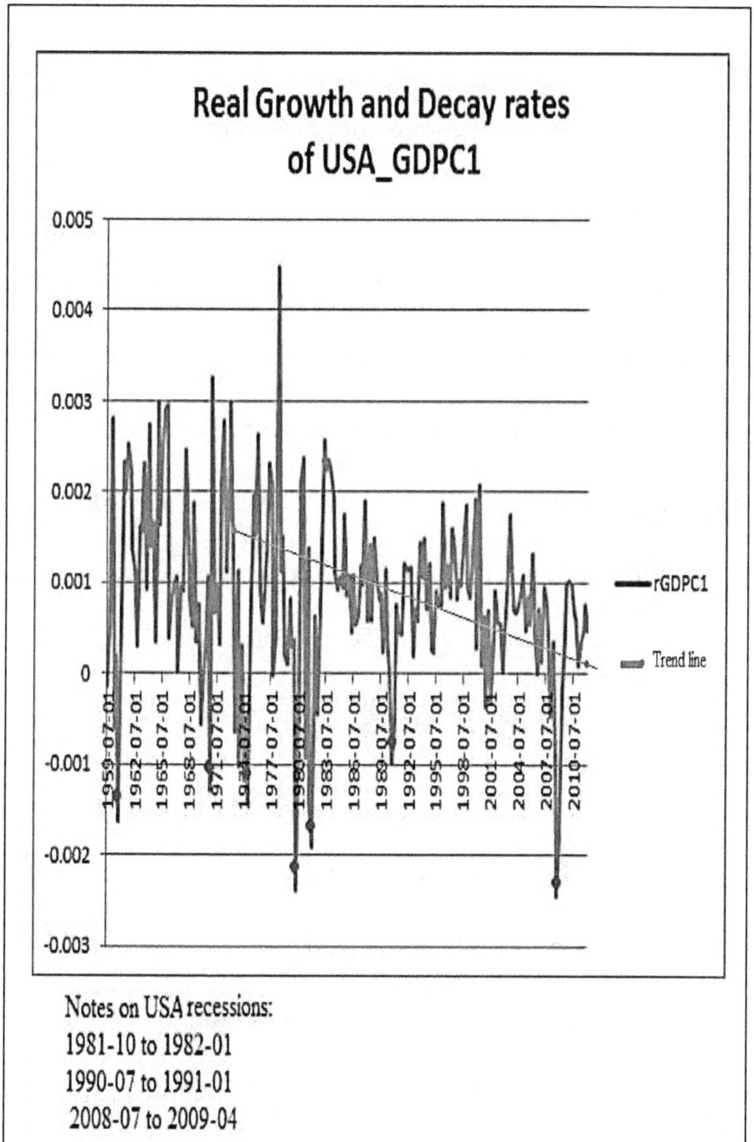

Figure 13, Growth, decay rates of real GDP, 1959- 2012.

Even when the process of wealth creation through jobs, had become uniquely deterministic to survival of for the middle class, they are frozen or become hostage to anonymous procedural-holds.

The economic wisdom and knowledge of wealth creation are confused with wealth holding, and not investments. Thus, totally relaying on private sector employments and investments have not been a wise one silver bullet choice, the under investment in infrastructures and government sector shown by lower government employments are consequential, too. They are shown in the correctable decay trends. The aggregate demand impacts are reflected in the lower current personal consumptions expenditures as well. The increase in the gap between the tax revenue and transfer payments are explained by tax policy shifts from high incomes to lower middle incomes.

In other words, a series of policy changes enacted since 1970s, under supply side mantras, and trickle down assumptions have proven to be wrong, because there has not been any policy mandate to monitor or link private sector employment and worker rights and income erosions, for their tax breaks. Some private sectors have taken advantage of quick technological injections and revenues bobbles to encourage wealth concentration and transfers. Thus, not only they did not encouraged or increased private employment, they under paid and avoided some taxes, thus governmental cyclical balancing act could not kick in, either.[18] That is neither Keynesianism nor Monetarism. It is looting. It is big businesses, mega multinational cooperation shirking ethical responsibilities, under any patriotic flags.

The average unemployment rates were calculated from monthly data.[19] The cooperate rate were assumed the highest rate given by IRS for cooperate federal taxes.

President Ronald Reagan tied tax rates (cooperate tax breaks) with job creation, his administration on economic advice, also threatened n a profit tax on cooperate on money-looting slackers to good effects. The deregulation policies and tax breaks in 2000 were not related to job-policies. Jack Abramoff court cases and book about lawmaking at federal level, and ALEC and cooperation's involvement in state law makings, and profit centers reveal new facts about American government.[20] Deregulation was a purposeful reregulation with specific commercialization designs.[21] The writing of laws and regulating them were relinquished to business interests and lobbyists to write or direct law making at federal and state level.[22] The insistence push to reduce the cooperate-tax rates to encourage employment is a myth. The logic is squeezed out of the political industrial complex. However, beyond a limited upper and lower band, it is contrary to Adam Smith golden hidden hand arguments, too. The greed has to be matched by regulation to curtail excessive self-harm and societal collateral damages.

The push for deregulation succeeded and it took a decade, but it inflected trillion dollars of global economic damages. It is astonishing that the greed and the statuesque cannot see facts as facts. The bad financiers can conjure and manufacture half-truths to fool and amaze the population to maintain them in their representative money positions. The American economy has been shocked and awed out of global economic leadership, jobs, and comfortable level of living. All cooperate-tax breaks that are without legal strings chaining them to decent jobs and average level of livings, present prime facie evidence of legislative and representational malfeasance.

In figure 14, the illustrations reflect the historical high tax rate, which were at 58 percent, now there is peculiar bickering, sequestrations, and inactions about paying a few percentages on the higher end of incomes.

Figure 14 shows average jobless rates per year, and cooperate income tax rates, 1948-2010. The graph vividly links the laws and tax breaks to unemployment trend lines.

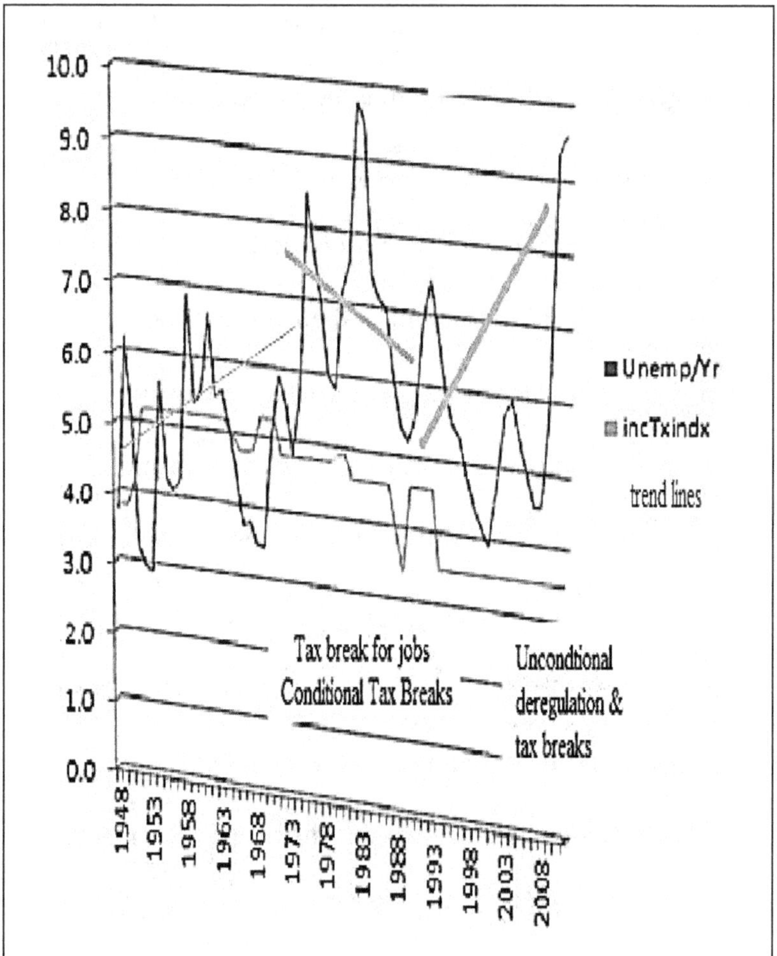

Figure 14, Av. unempl. rates, & Co. tax-rates 1948-2010.

All the time the cooperation and wealth concentrators benefited from technological injections, they were failing educational, structural infrastructures, student and graduates trainings, or employments, supplied by others, by a functional government, by immigrants' family, by the middle class American families. It is perfectly all right to quote authors long dead, even Adam Smith, if you have read the moral and ethical Adam Smith preceding his "Wealth of Nations," and the golden hidden hand.

Figure 15 shows us a comparative overview of American wages, benefits, and taxes, and the effect of inflation and families' demands in the real disposable income per capita graph.[23] The top graph shows the longer term, and the lower graph the shorter term for this millennium.

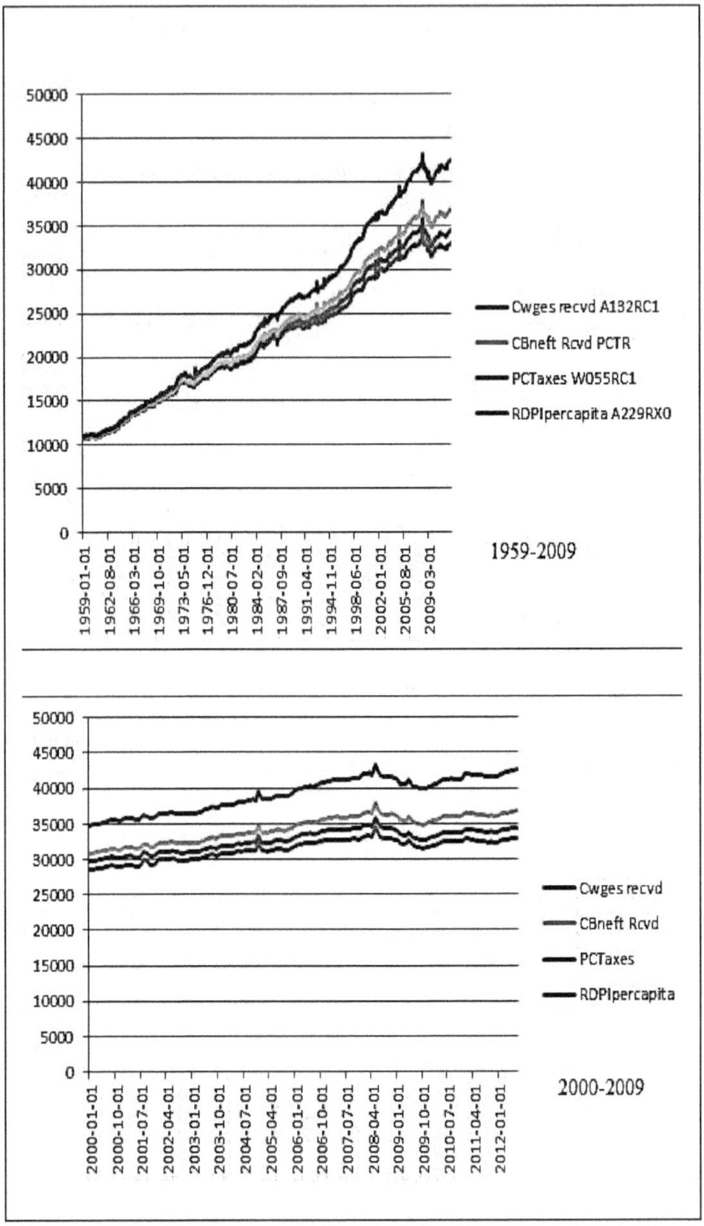

Figure 15, Nominal wages, benefits, taxes, RDI per capita.

Therefore, the implications of slowed economy in the level of livings are observed here visually.[24] The influence of slow growth on the wages and benefits and taxes are pronounced for the 2000-2009. Since last economic downturn in 2008, the impact shows more in the real disposable personal income per capita. Otherwise, the peril of knowing too little, combined with greed-centric lobbyists, and steroid-power of technological injections of modern political verbalisms have proven to be some of the main and more prominent reasons for chronic decay rates.[25] Failing to regulate private sector in their accountabilities to private job for their tax breaks are substantial. Ignoring proper cooperate-minimum tax-floors to balance their shortfalls in retention, retraining, and employment have been and will continue to be consequential. Blaming traditional but constraint educational systems for the clausal-coopered shortcomings and short-changing the employment systems, the wage earners are simply appallingly misguided.

It is true that free market economy system can outperform almost all other economic systems internationally, however, that is without market imperfections in economy or styles of governance, which would cheat the economic system from the supportive infrastructures, aggregate demand, and technological injections for imbalanced redistributions upward and wealth concentration. It will disable the tax-transfer and counter cyclical reparative fiscal corrections, with the bifurcated deregulated tax breaks unlinked from job creation. That is harm by policy not by chances, or economic faith and destiny. American economy optimistically can overcome these manufactured obstacles, and retain a more constructive growth path, again.

NOTES

[1] Bahman Fakhraie, Political Teconometrics, Utah, Ferdat Publishing 2012

[2] Bahman Fakhraie, *TECONOMIC ANALYSIS, ANALYTICAL ECONOMIC REMEDIES FOR THE POST-CRASH MILLENNIAL ECONOMIES*, Utah, Ferdat Publishing 2012

[3] This method, the formulation and graphics were developed and applied by Dr. Bahman Fakhraie 1970.

[4] You can follow the mathematic analysis in Appendix B, "Arithmetic of Work Hours."

[5] Follow the mathematic analysis in Appendix C, "Sustainability Conditions of Compensations."

[6] The neo-plutocracy reduced demand for domestic workers by estimated 30 percent, because, they outsourced and replaced them by technologies, or even cheaper, less regulated international workers in hinterlands.

[7] Ibid, you can follow this study more by using the following references.
Chiang, Alpha C., *Fundamental Methods of Mathematical Economics*, 2nd ed., New York: McGraw-Hill Book Company, 1974, 379-393.

Henderson, J. M. and Quandt, R. E., *Microeconomic Theory; A Mathematical Approach*, 2nd ed., New York: McGraw-Hill, 1972. 191-199, 279-282.

[8] Market imperfections influences the optimization analysis in Appendix A

[9] A comparative study shows a new index of 22 "rights to work," RTW states declined versus the 28 worker friendly states. These show 13.2 percent lower GDP per capita, 2 percent higher poverty rate, 3.1 percent higher median uninsured (health insurance) rate in RTW states. Darrell minor, Columbus State Community College, "Poverty and productivity", *neatoday*, Fall 2012, 40

[10] Bill Moyer and company, Untied State of ALEC, *PBS,* 2-http://billmoyers.com/episode/full-show-united-states-of-alec/

[11] Bahman Fakhraie, *Technological Injection, Dynamic New Capital Measurements and Production theory in Economics,* Utah, Ferdat Publishing 2012

[12] If you say free market alone or Keynesianism, you will find short tern solutions. Read (Teconomic, 2011).

[13] Money Zero Maturity is calculated by the Federal Reserve Bank of St. Louis. <http://research.stlouisfed.org/fred2/series/MZMSL>

[14] GDPC1, Gross Domestic Product, 1 Decimal, Seasonally Adjusted Annual Rate, Quarterly, Billions of Dollars, 1947-

01-01 to 2012-04-01, U.S. Department of Commerce: Bureau of Economic Analysis, Accounts of United States (NIPA).

[15] http://www.bea.gov/national/pdf/nipaguid.pdf), FRED, Federal Reserve Economic Data, Economic Research Division, Federal Reserve Bank of St. Louis, http://research.stlouisfed.org/fred2

[16] These are Author's calculation and graphs. other resources are from Economic Research Division, http://research.stlouisfed.org/fred2

[17] Ibid

[18] The most abused example is the capital tax rates (15 percent) used for employed billionaires' financiers. They should be taxed at current rates for financier employees at 25-35 percent for financial managers, CEO, and at 15 percent for retirees, savers, none financiers. This is, the now famed secretary-boss tax difference example.

[19] IRS and federal aggregate data plus authors' calculations were added; therefore the data for the graph have been modified from actual data.

[20] These are two versions, proofs of dynamic evolutions in these embedded malicious political-commerce interests, http://www.google.com/url?sa=t&rct=j&q=&esrc=s&source=web&cd=8&ved=0CFIQFjAH&url=http%3A%2F%2Foversight-archive.waxman.house.gov%2Fabramoff%2Fdocs%2Fabra

moff.pdf&ei=dLFnUP2MOeTjiAKvsoGoAw&usg=AFQjCNGQfUkZO5pHIBENdv3ISFZkFrrEcQ

[21] Jack Abramoff court cases and book about lawmaking at federal level, and ALEC involvement in state law makings, and profit centers reveal new facts about American government. The cooperation model laws and public representatives have formulated laws and profit centers in these areas, in education, incarcerations centers, and criminalization of immigration for profit. These are two versions, proofs of dynamic evolutions in these embedded malicious political-commerce interests, Ibid.

[22] Bill Moyer and company, Untied State of ALEC, *PBS,* http://billmoyers.com/episode/full-show-united-states-of-alec/

[23] Economic Research Division
Federal Reserve Bank of St. Louis,
http://research.stlouisfed.org/fred2

[24] Real Disposable Personal Income per capita, (RDPIPC) chained 2005 dollars, monthly,
seasonally adjusted annual rate.
Personal current taxes, billions of dollars, monthly,
seasonally adjusted annual rate
Personal Current Transfer Receipts (PCTR),
billions of dollars, monthly,
seasonally adjusted annual rate.
Compensation of employees, received, wage and salary,
private industries billions, of dollars, monthly,
seasonally adjusted annual rate.

[25] Bahman Fakhraie, *TECONOMIC ANALYSIS, ANALYTICAL ECONOMIC REMEDIES FOR THE POST-CRASH MILLENNIAL ECONOMIES*, Utah, Ferdat Publishing 2012

CHAPTER 4

CONCLUSION AND SUMMERY

Some of the more circular and problematic arguments have not produce any viable long-term solutions out of the millennial cyclical economic funks. The attempts to find an economic growth path out of modern cyclical macroeconomic difficulties have become voluminous. In this study, the more holistic unorthodox teconomic solutions have been advanced to find certain possible pathways out of the economic manufactured conundrums.

THE MILLENNIAL TAUTOLOGY, CONUMDRUMS AND MONETARISM

Parroting late Dr. Milton Friedman, University of Chicago is fantastic and all goes well in normal times, until one falls into the liquidity trap, and does not have any idea how to get out of the trap, thus the modern monetary tautology syndrome.[1] Then we need to hire a holistic economist, because blaming Dr. Friedman for recent macroeconomic fiascos will be a big economic whopper, even bigger than the myth of blaming John Maynard Keynes, six decades dead, for beltway dysfunctional abandonments of fiscal responsibilities.

The economists with political scientists, sociologist, and psychologists, Middle East Center are in the school of social and behavior sciences here at the University.[2] The millennial macroeconomics dysfunctional tautologies explain the recent macroeconomic fiascoes, and this holistic unorthodox presentation offers few solutions,

1. It makes a difference, if you employ people, or horde cash in cooperate multinational bank accounts, and in wealth concentrations. When the basic functional democracy, with decent wages and jobs redistributions, and functional laws of

commerce already exist, then (quantitative easing) QE (#3) becomes productive.

2. The employed are not all guards and gatekeepers, who block traffic and put fees or fines on commerce, and let people in and out of cooperate incarcerations camps. They are not all Mc-employees, or temporary workers with subminimum wage salaries, and inadequate or no health insurance or health care. Temporary low-wage employees, temporary workers work for limited hours, in order to remain unqualified for full benefits (healthcare, etc.). Others like the unpaid long-term interns, and graduate student workers are almost modern day peonage-workers, whom fall short of living wages, or any wages. All the time they have been student loaned to the financial size of a California Oceanside condominium. Nevertheless, the producers must keep products safe, children

educated and skilled-literate for existing commerce. The institutions and businesses ought to be willing to finish and polish those skills, and retrain the employees for their dynamic needs for technology literate workers, and sufficient sustainable demand. The supply sides drive technological alterations and injections to accommodate their improved commerce and expanded revenue, income and profits. Especially the technology sectors do not pay sufficient taxes to maintain the infrastructure they undermined and make obsolete regularly. The blame-the educators' mantras are perversely dishonest, and intellectually bent to shirk once nationally valued-ethical responsibilities. Like the unwillingness to employ and upgrade workers' skills, which have perverse elements of short-term gains, and long term nihilistic anti-intellectuality to it? Therefore, the institutions do not kill, pollute, poison, rob, cheat, discriminate, alienate, or scare the customers, and cause personal, firm, local, state, and federal bankruptcies (even for profit, or Schumpeterian short-term misnomers)!

3. You must have a functional democracy, which can employ people, rather than jump-off the cliff with them with new ill-timed austerity plans, which dismiss police, teachers, fire and mail persons, and professors to rob them of their pensions. On the other hand, they want to hoarse-trample, run over the elderly consumers, medically bankrupt them, and their grandchildren, and raise their entitlement age to after they die.[3] Most workers in hard toiled physical professions, machine shops, factories, petrochemical industries, agribusinesses are physical used up in their fifties. They can still stay productive with some medical attentions. Often, they are priced out in the imperfectly

noncompetitive health and insurance industries, and these industries paid political lobbyists in political offices. Alternatively, they want to replace educators, and other union workers, with jailhouse trainees in private arrangements and call it free market economics, borrowed from Stalin, old CCCP, and even older China, in a delusional attempt to compete with those decaying systems on the cheap, in a greed race to the lowest denominators of barely functional economic productions models.

4. Those with substantial income-revenues (cooperate entities, or some human automatons) have cheated the system. They paid negative (with subsidies) to 15 percent, instead 25-39 percent on multimillion dollars of executive level of salary-revenues, thus reducing government tax revenues. They transferred their shares of taxes to fees and taxes to

middle class, which they try to pay less wage-income, or dismiss them for well over three decades.[4] Therefore, the income-functionality depletes adequate demand out of the economic-systems, in this desperation time of need for cyclical-demand recovery pull. These poor conditions led to recent monetary conundrums, under the last few Federal Reserve Chairmen.

5. There must be a balance distribution of income earned, rather than wealth-concentrations. Therefore, between 1909-1929 USA-economy periods of wealth concentrations, and 1950s-60s economic growth periods, there were the (President Franklin Delano Roosevelt) FDR, two decades of increases and solidifications of economic and institutional job creations, higher incomes, and savings to encourage sustainable reparative cyclical recoveries.

6. Greed and short-term profit motives, monopolistic power concentrations, dismantling of bargaining tools, and use of international low-skill and low-wage comparatives to induce lower income at the middle and lower level of wage earners, while doing the exact opposite at higher end of income, and CEO and executive pays, have led to wealth concentration. They are the undoing forces of elemental FDR systems in the economy. That is where the tax revenues went in figure 12.
7. Those are elemental parts of gestalt that the necessary, sufficient, and sustainable conditions, which comprise the balance-functionality of macroeconomic dynamic conditions.[5] That best benefits the economy from technological injections strategies. Those comprise the balance to the functionality of macroeconomic conditions.[6]

8. It is paramount to recognize the co-dependencies of supply and demand, and elemental contributions of variables of production. Thus their equitable (if not equal, but sustainably) relative shares of national products injects higher velocity into the systems. In a manner, that allows dynamic technological injections. Human history is replete with bloviated bombast of wealth concentrators, unfortunately, also their blood, and massive damages to capital infrastructures, and national securities, which wiser societies with advanced cultures, established education systems tend to occasionally avoid. French revolution, American colonial wars (independence revolution), India independence wars, South Africa's old and new independence struggles, Iran 1950s, and Chilean recent post-colonial push for democratic independences are not

small trifles of modern civilizations that certain under educated shambolic historicisms imply.

9. These changes are dynamic (some time punitively recursive) in liquidity trap, employment growth, and full employment macroeconomic phases of functional democracies depend on their reparative healing phases. These conditions require different economic system-tools, even with technological injections raising employment in the liquidity trap.[7] These even in a market economy, are part of Dr. Bahman Fakhraie's solutions to Dr. Friedman's liquidity-trap tautology-conundrum.
10. These dynamic conditions of fiscal aggregations' data require different economic system-tools, even with technological injections for monetarisms, however, there are Nash, partial, and total equilibriums, stability, and sustainability and arithmetic and teconometrics gatekeeper markers

and bench-mark-holders. These mislead and misinform most sub-literate media experts on economics, and considerably more misinformed short-term bloviating financiers, and shambolic political polemicists. Their reelections, campaign donations and advertisement advances, their compliances, their votes, and their earmarked-laws are all in the mix. Imperfect competition in market can corrupt imperfect competition in democracy and political markets. Only the use of checks and balances, transparencies, and disclosures squeezes out human decencies, and the odd periodic theological compliances. All symbolic presentations of God, Allah are the most cheated and abused entities in modern human thoughts, with examples in all human endavers.

11. Monetary tools when pushing the string works. Fiscal tools when pulling the string is required are

mandatory and not optional. However, the system functionality must be primed. It cannot be with current student loan negative savings. That added to the mortgage shenanigan negative savings. On top of low wage low incomes few decades long, these gave you the current shambolic economic menageries you cannot shake. Depressions, recessions (double, or multiple dips), stagflation happen, when democracies go dysfunctional, even when on the right truck. Alternatively, political-party narcissism, Machiavellianism, and psychopathic interests can yield to abstractionism in face of mounting multiple war deficits and impact contradictorily on the economy. It is not the Federal Reserve every time. Despite the whipping boy status assigned to them, and to others, by the real guilty parties. Especially, when their last two main wars and many proxy wars have been unfunded war deficits (Go back to 10). Those shambolic abstractionists and obstructionists ignored the academic complexities of tax breaks, and admonitions of holistic unorthodox economists. Therefore, the inducements for job creation at the upper half of income earners for tax breaks saving were not implemented in the laws passed, just as they were forced under President Reagan administration. The tax revenues for adequate stimulus and government job creation were depleted, bloviating Keynesianism has been only a distraction for bumptious conservatism. Furthermore, stimuli and job injections with adequate real disposable incomes for demand-pull growth at the middle and lower income earners were perversely mischaracterized and abstracted.

12. Monetary-only policy is even a more advanced special case of dynamic aggregate data, which

depended on the value theory of micro underpinnings alterations. Pumping the prime pays off, if and only if, there is subterranean water in the system. (Go back to #1)

13. You can do QE # n, and still you will have the same problem. (Go back to # 8)
14. Hence, this is one of the more recent tautologies, or the millennial macroeconomic dysfunctional tautology conundrums.
15. One solution is a Fiscal Federal Reserve Board (**FFRB**) of economic experts (an addition to current Monetary Federal Reserve Board, **MFRB**) to deal with fiscal matters, taxation, honest budgetary prioritizations, even without changing the chair. The political entities have seen the lucrative aspect of these machinations and have fallen into dysfunctional anti-growth stalemates. Therefore,

their political aims have shut down the economic dynamism the system requires to function.[8]

16. The political bifurcated parties will draw salaries, pensions, benefits, but they shut down the economic functionality. They will set the given limited funds budgets. However, in decades, they will not be able to outspend the economy in harmful unfunded-adventures outside the country, and cause bankruptcy.[9] The harms are in symbiotic systems, which have morphed into dynamic systemic parasitic terminuses. They have indulged a 3 percent growth in military dependencies. While 1 percent growth in investments and income are barely registering to cover the expenditures of (not always), essential dependencies in defense (figure 5). While they all scream at the middle class benefits.

17. They could not channel funds into money-loops for friends, bank executive bonuses, or into foreign bank accounts. They have to evolve new tricks. They ought to become unable to block infrastructure expenditures for maintenances of the commerce, economic, and financial systems, which induces the desired natural rate of economic growth.
18. Perhaps because of modern stress-shocks and short memory issues of the voting public, which the late iconoclastic authors, Gore Vidal called "United States of Amnesia," and Studs Terkel (University of Chicago, 1934) referenced the vanishing senses of outrage and history, by noting, "The United States has 'a case of Alzheimer's."
19. When political operatives explain limits or correction of the 500 time higher econometrics mean of executive pays from average pays, as socialistic acts to see equal results, they are both

uninformed, and woefully under educated, or they are paid spinners. That is even more immoral than rotten cabbages. That is harming demand and investment side of supply (Go back to 10). It has to be acknowledged that descriptive Ayn Rand even combined with Hayak will not be suffusion to formulate the magic bullet solutions for immediate or short term relief. Those options do not exist.

20. The neo-plutocrats and neo-cons, the American Washington DC based neo-BenLadenists have baked the United States a depression in form of a new macroeconomic cake. They are fighting against monetary solutions, and delivering sub-intellectual paralysis, in the face of required fiscal actions. Here demagogueries of socialism, communisms, Keynesianism, and government programs in health, in education, in research and developmental technologies, even in infrastructural

maintenances and improvements are spread faster than an organic fertilizer-spreader can spread, without the holistic knowledge of proportionalities, or the enormity of nihilistic self-harm of inaction imposed on domestic economic conditions.

21. All you have to do is to vote them in this November election, or let the plutocrats purchase the other winning political party after the election, and go back to same old ways. It is your proactive voices and votes. No one will shake your duties off, do your votes, or alter you alertness status or dedication after the votes, or do both.
22. The wars will raise your deficit higher, take away your domestic capital formation, incomes, decrease government revenues, and therefore drop the potentials for new jobs. The neo-plutocrats and neocons will only make it harder for you to vote your votes now, if you let them. They even alter

bills, by late night earmarks, or make slight alterations between committees, houses, and use state functionaries. Their honorable intent (if honestly uninformed) has proven to be counterproductive to security of great many people, and this great nation. (Go back to #7)

23. Other new democracies, which like to mimic or duplicate USA democracy and constitution should study the pitfalls, and mind the Supreme Court justice Ruth Ginsberg's admonitions. This caravan road is long, winding, and planted with highwaypersons of questionable characters shape shifting into forms of friend and foes.
24. Teconomic lesson learned here is that certain global economies can utilized these technologies associated with extra words beyond conflict and wars verbigeration to expand job-creations, economic viabilities, increase money velocity, and

circulatory powers of sustainable distributions and teconomic growth in domestic economies, with diplomacy that garnishes international-trade, finance, and commerce.

Those economies will do much better with the technological injection, while other economies will linger with stagflations, and in certain cases follow debilitating even with slower growth rates, or long periods of decay. The states of global economies are at such condition now that slower growth will feel like decay comparatively.

SUMMERY

This study of Teconomic of Verbalism is part of holistic unorthodox analysis, which started with data of the exponential explosion of words used in United States. The expansions of technologies from prints on the cave walls, writing to prints duplications in mud spheres took evolutions in methods, skills, and tools that expanded before 6000-3000 BC, to 600 AD. The diffusion in technologies in paper travelled from 600 to 11,000 AD. The clustering of technological injections took a longer time, but creation, innovation, and expansion of technologies leading to the process of book prints took hold in 11000 to 13000. The process of book printing has expanded since 1300. We add the recent expansion of digital and electronics communication devises as in mobiles, and cell phones from 1970s to 2012, the estimation of 16000 trillion words used in United States by 2015 may prove to be an understatement. However, their significant historic alterations in human experiences are imprinting lasting international expressions, in finance, in economic experiences, in governmental organizational arrangements and relations, domestically and internationally. Therefore, proof of our initial statement is solidified again. That the Teconmics of Verbalism synthesizes the trifurcated forces of governances, finance, and economic markets and their global technological interdependencies in order to exerted inordinate forces to shape societal constructs, in modern times.

However, the needs for these technological injections do not elude other cultures. The synthesis of trifurcated forces of governances, finance, and economic global markets and their global technological interdependencies have exerted inordinate forces in modern times. It is very important to garnish this study and research equal to their global prominence and importance.

Therefore, the value theory of economic variables and conditions, which influence the aggregated data in fiscal economics, can become comprehensible to the practitioners in all three fields. Furthermore, it is important to realize scientific bases that will serve to construct our future systems on firmer foundations stronger than words of conflicts, with structures, organizational coordination and planning, and leadership to accomplish them.

The important Teconomic lesson is which global economies can utilized these technologies to expand job-creations, economic viabilities, increase money velocity, and circulatory power of international trade, finance, and commerce, in order to enable the entrepreneurial economic power houses embedded in their human capital, the most ubiquitous and renewable resources. The free market economy systems can outperform almost all other economic systems internationally. However, that is without market imperfections in economy or styles of governance, which would cheat the economic system from the supportive infrastructures, and complimenting solutions. The trifurcated forces of governances, finance, and economic markets and their global technological interdependencies have exerted inordinate forces in modern times. They can disable the tax-transfer and counter cyclical reparative fiscal corrections, with the bifurcated deregulated tax breaks unlinked from job creation and toward wealth concentration instead of wealth creation. That is harm by policy not by chances. Since there are clear disadvantages to certain economies, which underutilizes their people, their capitals, (human, and tangibles), or constantly perpetuate aimless aggressive wars. Therefore, those economies that better utilizing the political teconomic comparative analysis and utilize the expanded words beyond bloviated verbigeration will do comparatively better. They ought to allow themselves the wisdom to try for better.

§§§ THE END §§§

NOTES

[1] This research was finalized on Dr. Friedman 100-Birthday Memoriam, and it studies aspects of Monetarism, and its impact on this study."_THE MILLENNIAL MACROECONOMIC DYSFUNCTIONAL TAUTOLOGY CONUMDRUMS AND MONETARISM"

[2] University of Utah, have great students and professors,, they keep and lead many scientific fields and endeavors.

[3] Dr. Bahman Fakhraie, *TECONOMIC ANALYSIS, ANALYTICAL ECONOMIC REMEDIES FOR THE POST-CRASH MILLENNIAL ECONOMIES*, Utah, Ferdat Publishing 2012

[4] They also want to use austerity plan to remedy the financial deficit they have caused during the last term of a minority president. Last chance to pass it on to the middle class, while they can blame the backlash on someone else than the major investment bankers, CEOs, and cooperate strategists, lawyers, and financiers, patriotically.

[5] Dr. Bahman Fakhraie's current 4-books, check notes, promos, and references

[6] Bahman Fakhraie, *Technological Injection, Dynamic New Capital Measurements and Production theory in Economics,* Utah, Ferdat Publishing 2012

[7] This is Dr. Bahman Fakhraie's solution to late Dr. Friedman's liquidity-trap tautology conundrum. This is part of the intellectual negates about finding solutions to monetary macroeconomic problems, which came out of then a short private discussion with Late Dr. Milton Friedman at Utah State university, Logan Utah, on his way from University of Chicago, to University of Standard at Palo alto, California 1970s.

[8] This is an advanced holistic view, based on science and art of teconomics (holistic unorthodox economics), since before Adam Smith's other works and "Wealth of Nation," it showed up in periodic empires, and dynastic states spread around the globe.

[9] Dr. Bahman Fakhraie, *TECONOMIC ANALYSIS, ANALYTICAL ECONOMIC REMEDIES FOR THE POST-CRASH MILLENNIAL ECONOMIES*, Utah, Ferdat Publishing 2012

REFERENCES

Dr. Fakhraie, Bahman, "The Demand, and Supply Sides of Appropriate Technological Advancement," (Research paper at University of Utah Economics Dept. 2003)

—. *Technological injection, dynamic new capital measurements, and Production Theory in Economics*, (Michigan: ProQuest LLC, 2010) and, https://order.proquest.com/OA_HTML/pqdtibeCCtpItmDspRte.jsp

—. "Economic Theories and Practices in Technological Changes, capital measures, and Production." (Research paper at University of Utah Economics Dept. 1988)

—. "Hallowing headless nations? The need to invest on public education under the 1980s international economic conditions," (Research paper at University of Utah Economics Dept. 1988)

—. "Transfer of Technologies and Socioeconomic Theories of Dualism," (Research paper at University of Utah Economics Dept. 1983)

—.Technological Injection, Dynamic New Capital Measurements and Production theory in Economics, Utah, Ferdat Publishing 2012

—. *TECONOMIC ANALYSIS, ANALYTICAL ECONOMIC REMEDIES FOR THE POST-CRASH MILLENNIAL ECONOMIES*, Utah, Ferdat Publishing 2012

—. *THE DEMAND AND SUPPLY SIDES OF APPROPRIATE TECHNOLOGICAL ADVANCEMENT*, Utah, Ferdat Publishing 2012

—. *TECONOMICS, THE MICROECONOIC ANALYSIS, Scientific Synthesis of Microeconomics, mathematics and statistical, methodologies and technological parameters in production in Teconomics,* Utah, Ferdat Publishing 2012

Friedman, Milton and Schwartz, Anna Jacobson, *The Great Contraction 1929-1933*, vol.2, 2nd ed., New Jersey: Princeton University Press, 1973

Henderson, J. M. and Quandt, R. E., *Microeconomic Theory; A Mathematical Approach*, 2nd ed., New York: McGraw-Hill, 1972.

Mckinsey report, "Americans are exchanging ever more words," The Economist online, Aug 22nd 2012, 14:07, http://www.economist.com/blogs/graphicdetail/2012/08/daily-chart-5,

Samuelson, Paul Anthony, *Foundations of Economic Analysis*, New York, Atheneum, 1976

APPENDEX

A

ARITHMATIC OF OPTIMIZATION

The series of mathematical analysis are presented henceforth, to study utility optimization and demand side, and production optimization and the supply side analysis, author calculated these relations and formulations.

The traditional mathematical evaluation for optimization analysis is as follows. The optimization of traditional production function study is first under growth and decay condition. Dr. Bahman Fakhraie In appendix B presents the arithmetic of work-hours constrains. In C sustainability of compensation, and in D, traditional and logarithmic formulas of growth and decay are presented.

Traditional productions function,

$$o = f(v_i^\varepsilon)$$

Necessary condition, it is also known as the first order condition (FOC):

$$f'(v_i^\varepsilon) > 0$$

Sufficient condition, it is also known as secondary condition (SOC):

$$f''(v_i^\varepsilon) > 0$$

The traditional production function is with mathematical evaluation for optimization analysis.

Conditions in Case of Growth

$$o = f(v_i^\varepsilon)$$

Necessary condition:

$$f'(v_i^\varepsilon) > 0$$

Sufficient condition:

$$f''(v_i^\varepsilon) > 0$$

Implication: the function is positive and increasing at the increasing rate.

Condition in Case of Decay

$$o = f(v_i^{\delta})$$

Necessary condition:

$$f'(v_i^{\delta}) > 0$$

Sufficient condition:

$$f''(v_i^{\delta}) < 0$$

Implication: the function is positive and increasing at the decreasing rate.

B

ARITHMATIC OF WORK HOURS

This is the demand and utility optimization of individual about the use of daily time.

Assumptive conditions: s = 8 hours, after eight hour of, s, sleep, e is for education, and W is for work. Therefore, e and w share up to 16 hours, given, r, for wages.

$T = Te,w + S = 24$ hours

$Te,w = 24 – 8 = 16$ hours

Y, income is wage r, times the work hours, W. Utility is a function of education and income.

$$Y = rW$$

$$U = E * Y$$

$$U = (Te,w - W) \,.\, rW = 0$$

$$r\,W\,Te,w - r\,W^2 = 0$$

FOC

$$\frac{\Delta U}{\Delta W} = r\,Te,w - 2rW = 0$$

$$W = \frac{Te.w}{2}\ ,\ 16 > Te,w > 0$$

SOC

$$\frac{\Delta U^2}{\Delta W^2} = -2r < 0$$

From the FOC, given r=1, W ≤ 8 hours of work.

In the next section, given W is fixed, the increased in r, allows for out-shift in production.

LAGRANGE ANALYSIS OF N-VARIABLES

Lagrange analysis of n-variables and multi-constraints Lagrange multipliers are presented next.

$$f(X_S X_E X_W) = Q_i$$

$$g(X_S X_E X_W) = 24$$

$$h(X_S X_E X_W) = y_0$$

$$Z = f(X_S X_E X_W) + \mu[(24 - g(X_S X_E X_W)] + \gamma[(y_0 - h(X_S X_E X_W)] = 0$$

$$Qi = f(Xi)$$

$$g(Xi) = 24$$

$$h(Xi) = y_0$$

$$Z\mu = 24 - g(Xi) = 0$$

$$Z\gamma = y_0 - h(Xi) = 0$$

$$Zi = fi - \mu\, gi - \gamma\, hi = 0$$

Arithmetical Proof:

FOC

$$\vartheta Z^1 = 0$$

SOC

$$\vartheta Z^2 < 0$$

All constants are great than zero.

A good example of that above case is presented to the entrepreneurial time-limit decisions. Therefore, The Lagrange analysis of n-variables and multi-constraints Lagrange multipliers presented is the mathematical analysis of productive use of entrepreneurial times, on daily bases. Individual entrepreneurs have to make decision in time-use management, between productive choices they have to make in use of the fixed 24 hours. They make assumptive choices about their time uses, for required sleep, and time lot spent on education, and required work for income, as the relations showed.

C

GAINS MAXIMIZATION VALUE OPTIMIZATION

Budget determines expenditure on costs of production of X, and Y. λi is unit costs.

$$B = \lambda 1\ X1 + \lambda 2 Y2$$

S denotes level of skills, technological injections required.

$$S = s1\ X2 + s2\ Y2$$

Education and retraining required in use capital productively.

$$E_k = e1\ k_X + e2\ k_Y$$

Production function is,

$$Q = f\,(X, Y:\ \dot{B}, \dot{S}, \dot{E})$$

The Lagrange equation is,

$$Z_Q = f\,(Vi) + \mu i\,[(\dot{B} - \lambda i\ Vi)] + \mu j\,[(\dot{S} - \lambda j\ Vj)] + \mu l\,[(\dot{E}_k - \lambda l\ Vl)]$$

FOC

$$d\,Z_Q/dt = 0$$

SOC

$$d^2 Z_Q\ /\ d^2 t < 0$$

More assumptive conditions are as follows,

All constants > 0

OPTIMIZATION Of VALUE

Optimization of Value Ψis a function of maximization of profit, minimization of costs, and optimization of social welfare function Vi.

$$\Psi = f\,(\mathrm{Max}\pi,\ \mathrm{MinC},\ \mathrm{OptUi})$$

$$Ui = f\,(qxi,\ qyi\!:\ C\,(vi),\ Bi,\ \xi(-/+\ \text{or?}))$$

And

$$\Delta\ Ui = f\,(+,\ 0,\ -/+\ \text{or?})$$

COMPENSATORY SUSTAINABILITY Condition

Individual Utility function

$$\Delta\ Ui = f\,(+,\ 0,\ -/+\ \text{or?})$$

The utility of individual Vi is improved in consumption of Qxi, while the consumption of Qyi stays the same, and the budget line can improve, stay the same, or become negative, thus also influencing the utility function, allowing for other motivational multipliers, including ethical or moral factors endogenously or exogenously relevant to the decision matrix.

Social Welfare Function of Group Utilities

Opt SWFvi, SWFvi = f (Ui, Uj, Ul, Uξ (-/+?))

Majority of group utility will be better off at a new position A, therefore, they will agree to the project. The utility of some of group utility will stay the same. They stay either satisfy or join the last groups at position B. The utility of some of group will be worst off, there has to be tradeoffs, as in exchanges, higher remunerations, or tax-transfer strategies to optimize the experiences of all involved for them to agree to move to the better position A. This is another clause added to the arguments for sustainability conditions in all economic system orthodox or unorthodox, holistically.

SUSTIANABILITY CONDITIONS of COMPENSATIONS

Let us take a little time to study some of the sustainability conditions of compensations, with respect to social welfare functions for the group utility functions, for all individual in the group.

Two positions are A, and B, such that A is better than B.

$$A > B$$

Therefore, A is preferred to B,

$$\therefore\ A\ P\ B$$

$$SWFvi = f\,(Ui, Uj, Ul, U\xi\ (-/+?))$$

The compensatory sustainability conditions are as follows,

1. Sustainably condition universal criteria, it is if at least one individual utility function improves at A, others feel no change, then →A, A>B.
2. Sustainably condition Kaldorian criteria, this is when those in position A, pay, bribe, exchange with losers for the move to A, since and A P B, then A > B.
3. Sustainably condition Hicks criteria, those losing from move to A, cannot bribe the groups

to keep them from moving to A, therefore APB, →A, A>B.

4. Sustainably condition Scitovsky criteria, if the gainers can compensate some of the losers, and some of the losers cannot bribe any of the winners from the move to A, the move will take place. Such that A P B, hence, →A, A>B.
5. Sustainably condition Dr. Bahman Fakhraie criteria, or the dynamic sustainably universal criteria, that technological injection will improve all utilities positions proportionally, such that [∀ Ui at A] P B, then →A, A > B.

Students of economics may want to follow this study by reading Dr. Bahman Fakhraie reading list and other publications. There are more study under welfare economic theory, and potential economic dissertational works. Because there have been arguments about implication of nontangible in decision matrix, hint ξ (-/+,?), the issue of nonmonetary factors in utilities and social welfare function were injected here for the first time in history of economic doctrine.

D

RATES OF GROWTH AND DECAY

$$r^* = (Xt2 - Xt1)/Xt1$$

$$r = \frac{\ln Xt2 - \ln Xt1}{lnXt1}$$

$$Ey, ms = \frac{\frac{\delta y}{\delta t}}{\frac{\delta ms}{\delta t}}$$

E

ECONOMIC DATA REOURCES

GDPC1, Gross Domestic Product, 1 Decimal, Seasonally Adjusted Annual Rate, Quarterly, Billions of Dollars, 1947-01-01 to 2012-04-01, U.S. Department of Commerce: Bureau of Economic Analysis. Accounts of United States (NIPA), (http://www.bea.gov/national/pdf/nipaguid.pdf), FRED, Federal Reserve Economic Data, Economic Research Division, Federal Reserve Bank of St. Louis, http://research.stlouisfed.org/fred2

Economic data sources: Department of Commerce: Bureau of Economic Analysis. Accounts of United States (NIPA), (http://www.bea.gov/national/pdf/nipaguid.pdf), FRED, Federal Reserve Economic Data, Economic Research Division, Federal Reserve Bank of St. Louis, http://research.stlouisfed.org/fred2

CURRICULUM VITA

Bahman Fakhraie, PhD, UOU, UT, USA

University Of Utah, Economic Dept., U. O. U.; Salt Lake City, Utah USA, 84112

Permanent Address: c/o 1120 Canyon Rd #29; Ogden Utah 84404

E-Mail: bf9@utah.edu , bahf.econ@gmail.com, dr.bahf.econ@gmail.com

Honors and Awards:

Omicron Delta Epsilon Honor Society

Utah State U. USA,

Certificates Keys to Agricultural Development at the Local Level

Student Leadership Positions: **President of International Student Association** [ASUSU]

Bachelor of Science: Utah State University

Master of Science: Utah State University

PhD, University of Utah University of Utah

PhD, Economics (international economics), University of Utah

Certificate of Completion, PhD in Economics University of Utah, 2010

Certificate of Completion, PhD in Economics University of Chicago, 2011

Mission Statement:

To formulate optimum functionality in management teams, in order to make profitable and beneficial contributions, and create opportunity for merited advancements.

Utilizing rare combination of theory and empiricism, cultivated in multi-cultural inclusive settings in academic and private enterprise enhance the productivity and completion of project management.

Experiences, among fields of International Trade, Managerial, and Production theories in Economics, Finance, and Business, which modern business and academic institutions find very expensive to employ and too costly not to employ. The extensive background helps advance research in my field of study.

Goals:

I have initiated, passed, and funded many constructive projects --goals by committees--, where it has been value enhancing and mutually beneficial individually, and by team assists. Private Senior Economist: Research Positions with Contracts, Teaching, Research, Books, with contract.

Short Term Private Contracts are for economic and financial educational consultations.

Academic Preparatory Continuum:

PhD, University of Utah, Dissertation:

"TECHNOLOGICAL INJECTION, DYNAMIC NEW CAPITAL MEASUREMENTS AND PRODUCTION THEORY IN ECONOMICS"

Thesis statement:

The dynamic influences of technology and elemental factors of production --defined and measured in this dissertation-- are greater than commonly have been calculated or expected. The impacts of different measurements of capital stocks (traditional and new adjusted capital) on embodied and disembodied technological variables, on productivity, and economic growth of national social products are tested. The econometric effects of two new capital stock measures introduced in the writing of Friedrich August Von Hayek, John Maynard Keynes, and further developed by Evsey D. Domar, and ignored by most modern economists are examined. Therefore, we focus on the demand and supply side of technological embodied in capital, in human skill and produced goods and services, and the economy. Dr. Bahman Fakhraie's Book-link is at, https://order.proquest.com/OA_HTML/pqdtibeCCtpItmDspRte.jsp

Post-Doctoral Research and Goals:

1. Updating the econometrics of the dissertation to most recent available data and dates, (per available grants)
2. Include, countries, with acceptable data in the study, set up formulaic development in excel etc. for use. (per grants)
3. Focus on the theoretical advancement in production processes for systemic innovational additive methodologies, in Movie production, Agriculture, and other creative industries, using existing or newly hired faculties, in anchored and linked institutions. This is a great serious work in shadows of Adam Smith, Schumpeter, Hayak, and Keynes.

4. Stream line methodologies, and project for PhD Students, master students, and introductory fields' level, an extension of the dissertation and current copyrighted writings.
5. A multimedia production of Dr. Fakhraie's recent research,

NEW DYNAMIC ECONOMIC MODELS TO STUDY TECHNOLOGY INJECTIONS & DYNAMIC CAPITAL FORMATION, IMPACTS ON INTERNATIONAL TRADE, EXCHANGE RATE, AND GLOBAL ECONOMIC OPTIMASATION

Presentation by Dr. Bahman Fakhraie

6. Of course, this will be under Sec G of private contract and without infringing on rights of marketing, publishing, and distribution of the same. Certain contracts will be more restrictive, including specific names.

7. Finish the books series in post dissertation Teconomic studies, Micro, Macro, Teconometrics, Teconomic Analysis, and Political Teconomics. (in progress)

Books, published:

- Technological Injection, Dynamic New Capital Measurements and Production theory in Economics,
- TECONOMIC ANALYSIS, ANALYTICAL ECONOMIC REMEDIES FOR THE POST-CRASH MILLENNIAL ECONOMIES
- THE DEMAND AND SUPPLY SIDES OF APPROPRIATE TECHNOLOGICAL ADVANCEMENT
- TECONOMICS, THE MICROECONOIC ANALYSIS, Scientific Synthesis of Microeconomics, mathematics and statistical, methodologies and technological parameters in production in Teconomics

Production theory in Agriculture

Agro-production, Sheep production in Iran (an onsite research project 1975)

Monetary Macroeconomic Specialization (Milton Freedman,)

International Monetary macroeconomic Specializations (Robert Mundell)

Fiscal Analysis of oscillatory modifications

Applied Agricultural production in developing economies

Inappropriate Technology Transfers by Corporations

In addition, dualistic induced instabilities in pre-democratic economies.

Certificate in Rural Development from Utah State University

Research Skills:

Statistical packages, data selection, analysis, and formulations.

Computer Languages, Spread Sheet Data Analysis, Writings

Multimedia & Creative Skills: Film and video production, CD: audio and video works

Languages: Fluent in English and Farsi, I can read and write some French, and Arabic.

Fluent in Dezfili Dari dialectic

[One of the earliest spoken languages]

Teaching Experiences:

University of Utah: macroeconomic and microeconomic: introductory course, and related mathematics.

Utah State University: Economic Department, Persian language, and cultural studies to faculty and students, and teaching assistance for Agricultural economics.

Volunteer Helping of other students

Student leadership positions AUSU, as an undergraduate

PROFESSIONAL EXPERIENCE:

Founder and Management of Money Wise Firm (A Private Financial Education Foundation for Personal Financial studies), 1970 to date

Volunteer work: President; V.P., and Treasurer of Cherrywood Association Inc., multimillion dollars project, (Different 3 year cycles 1980 to 1999, consultation to date)

Real Estate Investor and Renovations, General Manger, to date

Agribusiness management, owner manager

Auto Agency sale manager/sold

Auto shop management/sold

Numerous Volunteer Projects: planning, budgeting, contracting, and finishing.

Beside educational publications, and digital multi-media CDS, DVD formats, copyrighted at USA the library of congress.

Other Experience:

Budget Analysis, Budget Setting, Budget Forecasting, Asset Allocation Studies, Portfolio Analysis Studies, Saving (Goal Setting) Plan, Tax Management Studies, Risk/Reward Management and studies, Economic

Condition risk Analysis, Managerial Goal Setting and Project Production Process and Enactments.

Economic Topics of Research and Lectures:

Non-Marxist Revolutions in Middle East (Iran)

Economic and Indices (Measurement Issues)

Economic Theories of Technological Changes and Capital Measures

Technological Change, Growth Rate, and Capital Formations with US Data

Education and Taxation

Hollowing Headless Nations! Education Crisis

Technological Parameters Statistical Measurements

New Econometric Measurements of Capital in Production Theory

Reading (Economic, Science, Mathematics, Econometrics, Statistics, Mystery, Ancients), Films (art, industry), Jazz, Foreign Eclectics music, Fly-fishing.

BUDGETARY AND MANAGERIAL DIRECTIVES

FAKHRAIE EDUCATION RESEARCH

DEVELOPMENT AND TRUST

FERDT

FERDAT

Fakhraie Education Research Development And Trust

Organization, Fakhraie Bahman

Grant proposal by

Bahman Fakhraie, PhD, ©, ®, ™

Budgetary, Managerial Directive and Legal Clauses

Legal letter and charges for unauthorized information use.

Legal letter is in cases of e-fraud, misuse of firms' information, or harm under sec. G. All linked and relaying entities, institutions, governmental agencies are accountable no exception.

Dear Sirs, persons, INC., (illegal use of firms' info), your current bill is **$10,000, ≤Ceiling $60 mils.** On behalf of Dr. Bahman Fakhraie, FERDAT, and the firm, family trusts.

These are the current charges related to illegal e-fraud and all harmful misuse of firms information, after the first time we asked you to terminate all contract and remove our name, firms' name etc. on this date.

1-Illegal use, the unapproved initial use of firm's name, contact name, duns #, any and all information supplied to USA government for the sole purpose of firm doing business with USA government, grant.gov, and NSF, Universities, other governmental and tribal entities, and all grantors. Minimum charges are $10,000.00, up to the ceiling of $ 60 million.

2-Use of firm contacts, names, address phone #, TIN/#s, and any information related to that.

Minimum charges are $10,000.00, up to the ceiling of $60 mils.

3- Continuation after repeated formal request to terminate illegal actions, sending junk e-mail, junk mail, forcing this firm to send back, by mail and certified mail. Legal costs related to that.

Minimum charges are $10,000.00 per each event, up to the ceiling of $60 mils.

4- Interference with firm soul business, time sensitive writing of government and private grants, at grant.gov, and NSF, universities, private foundations, NGOs and all grantors, with 4.5 million dollars floor. The Minimum charges are 4.5 million dollars, up to the ceiling of $60 mils.

4- Absolute or required non-disclosures by the firm or Dr. Fakhraie will require pre-paid plan with minimum flooring pay. Flex-legalism targeted at the firm, or Dr. B. Fakhraie will be due cause for nonpaid termination by the same, and harm-terms of Sec G of private contracts.
6- Punitive damages are up to 60 million dollars, if you do not stop, after the first notification.
Please make an effort to pay your bill. There will be additional charges added and sent to you for each time you try to contact the same entities, after the same dated termination notices.
Dr. BF, this is part of the legal notices under sec G, or formal termination notice dates.

Section 1, Mission Statement
To formulate optimum functionality in management teams, in order to make profitable and beneficial contributions, and create opportunity for merited advancements, **to advance research** in my fields of study. Utilizing rare combination of theory and empiricism, cultivated in multi-cultural inclusive settings in academic and private enterprises, I enhance the management in productivity and completion of productive projects, or suggest corrective recursive evaluation and total quality control improvements.
Experiences, among fields of International Trade, Managerial, and Production theories in Economics, Finance, Personal Finance management, and Businesses, which modern business and academic institutions find very expensive to employ and too costly not to employ. My extensive backgrounds help me advance research in my fields of study.
Section 2, Budgetary Clause

* All initial dedicated deposits (inflows) will be transferred to a FREDT, or FREDAT business account.

* No allotments or contracts activity will take place, until full transfer of funds has taken place per contracts. The cash-accounting method is used for tax purposes.

* Alteration to submit to requirements and regulations will fully transfer all risks, fees, and penalties, and legal responsibilities, to the source of the requirements.

* There will be a minimum product list, or writing, or proposal-output for further research, which will be presented and agreed to at the initial phases.

* This will be the only output legally required at the end of contract, or at the end of grant periods.

* There is a managerial flow chart enclosed to enhance comprehensions of cash flow, read after the legal notes section.

Section 3, Managerial Clause

* Dr. Bahman Fakhraie will act as agent, manger, and soul administrator, Executives director, Principle Investigator PI for FERDT, FERDAT, Fakhraie Bahman Organization, with full rights to take legal action and make final settlement on its accounts.

* Dr. Bahman Fakhraie will act as agent, manger, and soul administrator for Fakhraie Bahman Organization, with full right to take legal action on its accounts.

* A general electronic bookkeeping is followed, on periodical bases, as grants require it. Current standard is quarterly, post full disbursements of grant funding. (FRR is required quarterly)

* Details, information, managerial technologies are legally protected, and no such disclosure will be made of the Organization, administrator, assignees, or representatives of FERDT, FERDAT, or Fakhraie Bahman Organization. All copyright materials are marketable, or further developed by Mr. Fakhraie. All existing rights are reserved.

* All informal and formal requests can be made by mail, or email.

* There is forfeiture of all advances, in cases of mortality, health, or attempt at disbarment, legal action, harm, against soul administrator, Fakhraie Bahman Organization, with full right to take legal action on its accounts.

* Any and all such request will have to forward additional funding for legal representations and undue imposition of

costs or harm, please read the legal note and sec. G. It will always apply.

* Alteration to submit to requirements and regulations will fully transfer all risks, fees, and penalties, and legal responsibilities, to the source of the requirements.

* The reviewers will have access to a portion of the progress.

* Full transparencies are practiced for authorized agents only, mostly through the internet, after proper signatures are obtained.

* All future development, educational development will have to be contracted, or signed out temporarily.

* All copyrights and proprietary rights are reserved, granted, accorded to Dr. Bahman Fakhraie, and his living trust.

* The final product in initial agreement will be shared with the grantors, after all the financial settlements have been met.

* PI, FERDAT; Dr. Fakhraie, Bahman

  Dr. Bahman Fakhraie, PhD, UOU, UT, USA
* Position Classification, Executive level I,

* Salary exceeds Fed Cap for private contracts.

* NSF ID, 000586796, Organizational ID Code, P 269878425

* Private for Profit Business:

* DUNS Number D&B # [redacted]89684,

* CAGE/NCAGE: [redacted]S3, Congressional Districts, UT_001

* Sec G of private contract always applies

* For other institutional DUNS, etc. Please, check cover letter, or contact PI. Thanks

* UOU PI Information(dated)

□ Federal Interagency Committee on Education (FICE) Code for the U: **003675**
□ EIN. TAX ID/TIN: **87-6000525**

☐ DUNS Num: **D & B #009095365**
☐ Cage Code: **3T 624**
☐ NSF Institutional Code: **36756000**
☐ NIH Institutional Code: **514002**
☐ Congressional District: **UT-002**
☐ Type of Organization: **State Institution of Higher Education**
☐ AAALAC Accreditation: **8 March 2000 - (Animal Resource Center Facilities and Programs Accreditation)**
☐ USDA Registration Number (Animal Subject): **87-R-0001**
☐ PHS Animal Welfare Assurance ID Number: **A3031-01**
☐ Human Subjects Federal Wide Assurance: **FWA00003745 (expires 11.06.2011)**
☐ Effective Date of Cost Accounting Statement: **Disclosure Statement submitted 12.31.97 (not yet audited or approved by**
* **DHHS)**

Section 4, Legal Clause, All Right Reserved & Other Legal Notes
All rights will revert to author after 3 years, if limited rights are contracted.

E. Speech, Lecture Tours, and Research Papers & Follow Up:
All publications or Grant-products are commonly published on completion, USA Library of Congress, Trade Journals, Or Author's websites, etc.
Contact for individualized contracts

F. For Time Donation, And Charity Events: 1. 5% of Net contracts paid 2. Time by Appointments Only.3. Write Donations Checks to Fakhraie Trust fund / Bahman Fakhraie

G. Any and All Risks or Harms invokes these legal clauses. The Following legal clauses are base minimum, and will not limit all rights and legal protection, with uniform constitutional rights they are implied and accorded. Contractually all rights are implied and accorded. Please, read all the legal notes before using any materials.

G1. In Cases of misuse of these materials, plagiarisms, use to put at risk of harm, or to harm, (Legal, or Etc.) the firm, CEO, FERDT, president: Mr. Bahman Fakhraie, His family members, it will result in $60 million legal action per each event in United States Courts/ any Jurisdictions determined or set by author or a trust set up by Mr. Bahman Fakhraie. Also, use of creative ideas and intellectual properties for any commerce direct or indirect or by proxy, expansions of outlines, attempts to defraud, over charge, harm with illegal acts, misuse of private and confidential materials, information, and properties, letters, checks, e-mails, faxes, any and all communications, and any electronically stored materials and pictures, or false claims against the above entities will be an agreement with and subject to all elements of this contract, and as a user license, without nullifying further and ensuing legal actions or collections, or as directed by the same or authorities. All other contracts are one-time contracts and s. t. this contract. Please, notify firm, Mr. Bahman Fakhraie, of all infractions, transactions, or transfer to individuals or to private or government entities in accord with current laws.

G2a. All Costs due to inquiries, related or required business licenses, legal paper works, and hours, all costs related to corrective or reparation publicity, bonding and insurances costs, stock related activities, all costs related to any harm (financial & legal) will be charges to the sources and inquirers, and none to the firm or Bahman Fakhraie, his family, or any and all of their related assets. All attempts to harm, engagements, cashing checks or accepting cash from the same entities is an agreement with all elements of this contract.

G2b. All copy rights associated with written works and further development of all works remains with the author Bahman Fakhraie or his trusts. All development rights are reserved by the same entities.

G3. Any and all unsolicited commercial phone calls, to Mr. Bahman Fakhraie and, his family will result to a minimum of $ 500 per call charged to the source, due and payable in the same month the call is made, all other elements of this contract also apply, all contracts remain subservient to this contract, all costs of collection and legal actions also are added to the bill payable by source and not Bahman Fakhraie and these entities.

G4.All Consultation and coaching involves risks due to market, business, political, etc. costs and damages related to all such risk are paid by individuals or business entities involved and none is implied or taken by Bahman Fakhraie, his family, or any related assets, under any and all conditions. These entities' court fees are $10,000; et minimum.

G5.Uncomfortable conditions, misapplications of any law to harm, harassment, odd-hour calls, etc will be due cause for termination of services without refund, and are actionable per this contract.

§§§§

All Right Reserved & Other Legal Notes

All publications or Grant-products are published on completion, USA Library of Congress, Trade Journals, Or Author's websites, etc. All rights revert to author after 3 years, if limited rights are contracted.

E. Speech, Lecture Tours, Research Papers & Follow Up:

1. Per Each Event-$ 350,000 +.
2. with Foreign Travel-$ 3,000,000
3. Book/Cash Advance $6,000,000; Net Royalties ~40%
4. Scripts: /Starting from....................$ 300,000
5. Movie Script (120+Pages)................$ 3,000,000
6. Or Cash Advance Plus 2% of All Gross paid annually
7. Consultations Fee/Initial charge non-refunded $ 10,000, & ...10 %
8. Business limited ventures, partnerships, etc. .... ≥ 30%
9. Salary executive level I

F. For Time Donation, And Charity Events: 1. 5% of Net contracts paid 2. Time By Appointments Only.3. Write Donations Checks to Fakhraie Trust fund / Bahman Fakhraie. G. Any and All Risks or Harms invokes these legal clauses. The Following legal clauses are base minimum, and will not limit all rights and legal protection, with uniform constitutional rights they are implied and accorded. Contractually all rights are implied and accorded. Please, read all the legal notes before using any materials. G1. In Cases of misuse of these materials, plagiarisms, use to put at risk of harm, or to harm, (Legal, or Etc.) the firm, CEO: Mr. Bahman Fakhraie, His family members, will result in $60 million legal action per each event in United States Courts/Jurisdictions determine by author or a trust set up by Mr. Bahman Fakhraie. Also, use of creative ideas intellectual properties, expansions of outlines, attempts to defraud, over charge, harm with illegal acts, misuse of private and confidential materials and properties, letters, e-mails, faxes, any and all communications, and any electronically stored materials and pictures, or false claims against the above entities will be an agreement with all elements of this contract, and as a use license, without nullifying ensuing legal actions or collections, or as directed by the same or authorities. Please, notify firm, Mr. Bahman Fakhraie, of all infractions, transactions, or transfer to individuals or to private or government entities. G2a. All Costs due to inquiries, related or required business licenses, legal paper works and hours, all costs related to corrective or reparation publicity, bonding and insurances costs, stock related activities, all costs related to any harm (financial & legal) will be charges to the sources and inquirers, and none to the firm or Bahman Fakhraie, his family, or any and all of their related assets. All attempts to harm, engagements, cashing checks or accepting cash from the same entities is an agreement with all elements of this contract. G2b. All copy rights associated with written works and further development of all works remains with the author Bahman Fakhraie or his trusts. All development rights are reserved by the same entities. G3. Any and all unsolicited commercial phone calls to Mr. Bahman Fakhraie, his family will result to a minimum of $ 500 per call charged to the source, due and payable in the same month the call is made, all other elements of this contract also apply, all contracts remain subservient to this contract, all costs of collection and legal actions also are added to the bill payable by source and not Bahman Fakhraie and these entities. G4.All Consultation and coaching involves risks due to market, business, political, etc. costs and damages related to all such risk are paid by individuals or business entities involved and none is implied or taken by Bahman Fakhraie, his family, or any related assets, under any and all conditions. These entities' court fees are $10,000; et minimum. G5.Uncomfortable conditions, misapplications of any law to harm, harassment, odd-hour calls, etc will be due cause for termination of services without refund, and are actionable per this contract.

§§§§

Letter of Agreement with FRDET and Fakhraie Bahman

I/We (Ms., Mrs., Mr.):
Business Name:
Social Security numbers: ..../......./............... ..../......./...............
Tax ID Numbers: ....
Driver License Numbers: ....
Passport (Birth Certificate) Numbers: ....

Have read all the information supplied by Mr Bahman Fakhraie, and /or FRDET (Trust, LLP). Agree to supply all correct financial and related information and select the following services by marking (X), or Letter a b c, Or Number 1 2 3, or write and specify. Agree to the power of attorney required to confirm or acquire financial and related information. Plus a check for $3000, for preliminary registrations, legal and financial inquiries, and licensing fees.

1: ☐ 2: ☐ 3: ☐ 4: ☐ 5: ☐ 6: ☐ 7: ☐ 8: ☐

Specify which kinds of the following accounts you will require:
Individual/Gov. ☐ Joints ☐ Joint with survival rights ☐ Trusts ☐
Details:

Business types:

Ltd Partnership (LLP, LLC) ☐ Soul Owner ☐ Inc/Gov ☐ Firm ☐

I/We agree to pay the fees and costs as they accrue, after 30 days a charge of %10 per annum is added to past due amounts until they are settled or paid in full. That at least 75% charges and expenses are paid no later than six month after initial reports or outlines are examined. That all travel lodgings and phone charges, legal research, and research hours, I/We request are fully paid. I/We have read and understand the nature of business, business cycles, market price fluctuation risks, currency fluctuation risks, social and political risks, natural and climatic risks, and all other risks herewith not itemized; therefore, I/we accept all financial losses, responsibilities, all punitive or compensatory damages that occur for all activities that are undertaken based on or claimed related to the report or reports, advise and etc., generated by Money Wise Firm, Bahman Fakhraie or all the entities named, agents, and associates. I/We understand in cases of any false, misleading, or withholding information the Money Wise Firm and all entities named above will not be held accountable, responsible, financially or otherwise, and will be refunded for any damages fully. I/We release all others associated with Money Wise Firm, and Bahman Fakhraie from financial losses, responsibilities, all compensatory and punitive charges concerning activities I/We undertake.

Sign (full name, titles, and address)

Business (Name, Address; Agents' title):

Details:

Sign (full name, titles, and address)

Section 5, Organization Chart

⇔Requests for grants, grant and contract proposals and Minimums contracted output Grant Funds,

⇓ Organization DUNS, University DUNS ⇓

Administrator ⇒FRDAT

FERDAT & FERDAT- C

⇓

Publishing and Production

President, Administrator, Executive level 1

⇓

Bahman Fakhraie, PhD, © 2011, UOU, UT, USA ®, ™

Tasks and controls, TQC, and Redo, Recycles

⇔Tax and expense disbursements

⇓

Completed project Vs. Minimums contracted output

⇔ Informal notification of source of funds, with future project proposal if any,

⇒Formal and final notification from FRDET, FERDAT

⇔ Final confirmation of conclusion from Administrators

⇒ Final confirmation of conclusion from Organization Fakhraie

⇔ Keeping communication and network open to future project.

Section 6, DATA MANAGEMENT:

Relevant data will be managed, and stored. Moreover, the data and the progression of data used will be stored post completion. As a common practice, Dr. Bahman Fakhraie will, also preserve a historical over view of data for legal purposes, for future use. A portion of that will be shared if requested in written form, post settlement of all expenses. The ethical requirements will be followed in accordance with the applied law established.

The final product will be shared with the grantors, after all the financial settlements have been met. The reviewers will have access to a portion of the progress. All publications or Grant-products are published on completion for academic and educational research, USA Library of Congress, trade journals, FERDAT Publishing, author's websites, other academic journals, etc.

All rights will revert to author after 3 years, if contract exits for limited rights.

Labor laws and benefit distribution will be according to the institutional Fed Cap limits, private contracts; vendors are responsible for their own legal obligations. (Publication Ink, FedExx, kinkcos, vendors etc.)

CPA and Legal establishment, outside to this entity will be contracted to handle more complex issues when they arise, all cost are due, prior to any such required actions are requested.

Full transparencies are practiced for authorized agents only, mostly through the internet, after proper signatures are obtained. All copyrights and proprietary rights are granted, accorded and reserved to Dr. Bahman Fakhraie,

All future development, educational development will have to be contracted, or signed out temporarily, they will revert to Dr. Bahman Fakhraie, in case of all legal issues.
These and other clauses will be amended and upgraded as required over time, they all apply.
Absolut or required non-disclosures by the firm or Dr. Fakhraie will require pre-paid plan with minimum flooring pay. Flex-legalism targeted at the firm, or Dr. B. Fakhraie will be due cause for nonpaid termination by the same.
G. Any and All Risks or Harms invokes these legal clauses. The Following legal clauses are base minimum, and will not limit all rights and legal protection, with uniform constitutional rights they are implied and accorded. Contractually all rights are implied and accorded. Please, read all the legal notes before using any materials.

Section 7, Vita

Bahman Fakhraie, PH.D. University Of Utah
Economic Dept., Salt Lake City, Utah USA, 84112
Permanent Address: c/o 1120 Canyon Rd #29; Ogden Utah 84404-7663
E-Mail: bf9@utah.edu , bahf.econ@gmail.com
Honors and Awards: Omicron Delta Epsilon Honor Society
Student leadership positions: President of International Student Association
Bachelor of Science: Utah State University
Master of Science: Utah State University
PhD, University of Utah University of Utah
Mission Statement:
To formulate optimum functionality in management teams, in order to make profitable and beneficial contributions, and create opportunity for merited advancements.
Utilizing rare combination of theory and empiricism, cultivated in multi-cultural inclusive settings in academic

and private enterprise, I enhance the management in productivity and completion of productive projects, or suggest corrective recursive evaluation and total quality control improvements.

Experiences, among fields of International Trade, Managerial, and Production theories in Economics, Finance, Personal Finance and Business, which modern business and academic institutions find very expensive to employ and too costly not to employ. The extensive background helps advance research in my fields of study.

Goals:

I have initiated, passed, and funded many constructive projects --goals by committees--, where it has been value enhancing and mutually beneficial individually, and by team assists.

Private Senior Economist: Research Positions with Contracts, Teaching, Research, Books, with contract. Short Term Private Contracts are for economic and financial educational consultations.

BOOK PORMOTIONS

The worst the economy gets the more you want to read, the scientific analytical reasons, why!

Dr. Bahman Fakhraie, PhD, Economics, University of Utah, Salt Lake City Utah, BS, and MS from Utah State University, at Logan Utah. Dr. Bahman Fakhraie dissertation adds to the influences and importance of the Unorthodox-Holistic Economic analyses, or the Gestalt of Unorthodox economic doctrine, in the millennial age of technological paradigm shifts. He is A Published Economist, Author, Researcher, Investor, and Private Contractor. His expertise are in international trade and finance, economic production, growth (theory and application), development theory, econometrics, (math, micro, and macro), Agriculture economics, and agronomy.
Books:

- Technological Injection, Dynamic New Capital Measurements and Production theory in Economics,
- TECONOMIC ANALYSIS, ANALYTICAL ECONOMIC REMEDIES FOR THE POST-CRASH MILLENNIAL ECONOMIES
- THE DEMAND AND SUPPLY SIDES OF APPROPRIATE TECHNOLOGICAL ADVANCEMENT
- TECONOMICS, THE MICROECONOIC ANALYSIS, Scientific Synthesis of Microeconomics, mathematics and statistical, methodologies and technological parameters in production in Teconomics

$89.99
ISBN 978-0-9852958-4-4
58999>
780985295844

www.ingramcontent.com/pod-product-compliance
Lightning Source LLC
LaVergne TN
LVHW022041200926
848481LV00003B/739